Also by Kathryn Petras and Ross Petras

Unusually Stupid Americans

The 776 Stupidest Things Ever Said

The 365 Stupidest Things Ever Said

The 776 Even Stupider Things Ever Said

The 776 Nastiest Things Ever Said

The 176 Stupidest Things Ever Done

Very Bad Poetry

Stupid Sex

Stupid Celebrities

Stupid Movie Lines

The Stupidest Things Ever Said by Politicians

Age Doesn't Matter Unless You're a Cheese

Here Speeching American

A Very Strange Guide to English as It Is Garbled Around the World

Here Speeching American

KATHRYN PETRAS

&

ROSS PETRAS

VILLARD / NEW YORK

LIBRARY OF CONGRESS CATALOGING-IN-PUBLICATION DATA

Petras, Kathryn.
Here speeching American: a very strange guide to English as it is
garbled around the world / Kathryn Petras and Ross Petras.
p.   cm.
ISBN 0-8129-7315-1 (pbk.)
1. English language—Errors of usage—Humor. 2. English language—
Foreign countries—Humor. 3. Communication, International—
Humor. I. Petras, Ross. II. Title.

PN6231.E74P47 2004
428'.002'07—dc22   2004042036

Villard Books website address: www.villard.com

Printed in the United States of America

2   4   6   8   9   7   5   3

Book design by Dana Leigh Blanchette

*To all of you
intrepid travelers out there,
recently (and euphoniously)
immortalized in an overseas
travel brochure as:
John and Jane Q. Pubic*

Contents

About This Book

When one travels abroad, one is met with English wherever one goes. Well, let us rephrase that. One is met with somewhat optimistic *attempts* at English.

Thus this book, *Here Speeching American,* a light-hearted examination of the new lingua franca—or, more aptly, lingua anglica fracta: Fractured English. Garbled English. Bad English . . . as spoken overseas.

Written in the form of a tongue-in-cheek travel guide, it dishes up not helpful advice, but rather, examples of the best or worst, as the case may be, of "English as she is spoke" abroad. All of the examples of fractured English are (most painfully!) true—plucked from actual hotel room signs, travel brochures, restaurant menus, advertisements, and more.

One quick note: We want to stress that language mangling is universal, and knows no specific country or culture. Native English speakers, of course, are guilty of the same egregious errors in foreign languages. (You should hear us order—or *attempt* to order—food in a Greek restaurant. As for French restaurants . . . well, let's not go there.) But that's another book. . . .

This particular book is an excursion into the twilight zone of perilously flawed *English* communication overseas. The reader is urged to follow the instructions seen on a Namibian road sign:

Danger Ahead
Fasten Safety Belts
And Remove Dentures

Introduction

So you're going abroad . . . or planning to. Or thinking that you might be going abroad someday. Sooner or later. Or, for that matter, perhaps you *know* someone who is going abroad . . . or planning to.

Your bags (or theirs) are packed and you (or they) are ready to go, as Peter, Paul, and Mary (among others) once said.

What else do you need but the right traveling companion? May we humbly suggest this guide?

It's a valuable "vade mecum," a better *Baedeker's*, a fun *Fodor's*. It guides you in your globe-trotting—and, better yet, it lets those overseas "locals" speak to you, the intrepid tourist, in their own words. They're your hotel concierges, your airline flight attendants, your guides, your waiters . . . your new foreign friends!

What better way to get to know the world than to travel? And what better way to travel *better* than to use this book! We'll take you step-by-step through your trip—from your flight to your hotel to local restaurants and sightseeing . . . and much more. We guarantee one thing: Wherever you're going, your trip will be filled with memories. Priceless memories. And so, let us leave you with this wish:

> May every memory bring the feeling that you have not lived for anything.
> > *translation enclosed with a piece of Chinese calligraphy for tourists, Hong Kong*

Bon voyage!

Here Speeching American

Air Travel

Your trip abroad often begins before you set foot in your destination country. We are speaking, of course, of foreign airlines. What better way to immediately get to know the people and the culture, and to get a glimpse of the fun times you'll soon be having, than flying on your host country's national carrier?

The first impression you'll get of the country you'll be visiting is from your flight crew. They are carefully selected to be the perfect ambassadors.

Duck feet? You're out. Pigeon toes? Out! Bow-legs, pimples, warts, moles, dark skin, scars, bad breath? Out! . . . [And] they must be virgins.

> *Hao Yu-ping, director of flight attendant school*
> *at China Air, describing the airline's*
> *requirements for flight attendants*

The stewardesses of Southwest Airlines must go through four steps, such as hardship, tiredment, dirt feeling. Beside the quality of general stew-ardess.

> *from the first edition of Chinese airline*
> *Southwest Civil Aviation's* Inflight Magazing
> [sic]

And they're trained to give you *exceptional*—even ex-otic—service.

Sir would you like some sauce on your balls?

> *Singapore Airlines stewardess, quoted in*
> *Singapore newspaper*

The crew will want to make your flight as comfortable and safe as possible, so read the helpful material in the seat pocket—and be assured of a relaxing, worry-free trip.

Bags to be use in case of sickness of to gather remains.

> *slogan on a Spanish airline's airsickness bag*

And an itch-free trip too!

> Dear Passenger,
> Wish you have a joyful journey!
> When you are in public talking and laughing and drinking and singing . . . living a happy life, suddenly you feel some part of your body is too itchy to endure. How embarrassed! Please dial fax 01-491-0253, you will gain an unexpected result.
> *Air China brochure*

You may want to read the specifics of your flight for further reassurance.

> International Fright Information
> *airline timetable, China Airlines in-flight magazine*

> Maximum cruising fright level
> *in-flight magazine, China Eastern Airlines*

So settle back and dip into that in-flight magazine. What a wonderful way to begin your vacation!

> Enjoy French odor in the South Pacific.
> *from a French airline (UTA) and government of New Caledonia ad*

We'd like to offer our affection as a gift by the white bird on sky to every genuinely go the same may together with you. This is our only requite to you.

> *dedication, Xiamen Airlines in-flight*
> *magazine, China*

Take this opportunity to read about the sights you'll soon be seeing.

Situated in the monsoon tropical zone, though the year covered with luxuriant vegetations, the land of Dai La by the Red River is "printed the forms of sitting tiger and winding dragon. . . . looking all over Vietnamese country, that's land of scenic beauty, an important metropolistes indeed for four directions to gatter and the first rank of city merined to be regarded as Capital forever."

> *in-flight magazine, Vietnam*

Incest sticks hang from the ceiling of a Taoist temple.

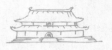

> Morning Calm, *in-flight*
> *magazine, Korean Air*

What an informative and exotic learning experience! And get ready for an exotic eating experience too! We're not talking little foil packets of Planters Peanuts . . .

Fduhy Sesane
China Airlines (CAAC) snack food

We will now be serving snakes.
Singapore Airlines stewardess,
quoted in Singapore newspaper

Near the end of the flight, you'll often be handed an immigration card. It's times like these you may find yourself wishing you'd paid more attention in eighth-grade French (not to mention Chinese).

Fill in the card clearly in the following languages: Chinese, English, French and Spanish. Japanese names shall be filled in Rome alphabet.
instructions on immigration form, China

And remember any special instructions about disembarking you may have received.

Upon arrival at Kimpo and Kimahie Airport, please Wear your Clothes.
on invitation to dedication ceremony from a Korean steel mill

IN THE AIRPORT

A foreign airport can be intimidating, but your hosts will do their best to make you feel completely at home.

> Welcome To A Great Stage Where
> Wings of the World Gather, Flap,
> and Fly skyward
> > *from a guide to Narita*
> > *Airport, Japan*

Speaking of flapping, you'll see many ads for exciting overseas airlines that might induce you to book another flight immediately.

> AEROFLOT: Introducing wide boiled aircraft
> for your comfort . . .
> > *ad for Soviet (Russian) airline*

> Akita to Okinawa
> Non-Stop Fright
> > *from ad for JAS airline, Japan*

> Air Vietnam: The most experimental airline
> > *slogan in 1960*

> Malaysia Airline. From Kuala Lumpur to Kuala
> Lumpur. Fair: 7,760 baht; US $310.
> > *ad in* Chiangmai Guidelines, Lao Aviation, Laos

Of course, the airport will offer the same efficiency you're used to at home.

>   Irregular Flight Service
>   *sign in Xian Airport, China*

>   ← →
>   This Way Please
>   *sign at Malé International Airport, Maldives*

But airport services may be a bit more *exotic*.

>   Shoe sunshine
>   *sign at shoeshine stand, Osaka Airport, Japan*

>   Make Tsogt Chandmani Currency Exchange your choice and take the advantage and the flavour with you.
>   *slogan of currency exchange, Mongolia*

>   Air India Passengers for Your Reading Pleasure
>   *sign in airport, Bombay*

Don't be too surprised if your Louis Vuitton isn't on the baggage carousel . . .

We take your bags and send them
in all directions.
> *sign in an airline ticket office,*
> *Copenhagen*

A little anticipation seems to be the rule of the day at
some airports.

Passengers expecting mishandled baggage should
obtain landing certificate from customs.
> *Government of India disembarkation card*
> *given to passengers upon arrival in New*
> *Delhi's airport*

Payment Before Ordering
> *sign at restaurant in Ben*
> *Gurion Airport, Israel*

Or sometimes not . . .

Buy ticket after normal time.
Flying off forward 30 mm transact
> *stand-by ticket window in Wuhan, China,*
> *airport*

Then it's on to customs. Entering a country can be a *tad*
tricky . . .

Objects must be declared. If there isn't any ob-
ject mark "X" only at the quantity "Yes" column

and if there are any objects, cross out letter "No" and at the same row write exact amount of weight of these objects in words or in figures.

customs form, which also warns sternly against "giving false declaration or having the action of tricking," Vietnam

. . . or, for that matter, leaving . . .

DISTINGUISHED VISITOR:
It is known that all the turistic services in Mallorca are maintaining a correct relation price quality, but even though, we wish to prize the establishments and services that to the opinion of our visitors, surpass notoriously for their quality.

To be able to fill out these questionnaires you must write the name of this establishment, installation or turistic service, as is shown below, and you must give a punctuation between 6 and 10 points hoping that the service that you must punctuate has been the best in the relation price-quality.

sign urging travelers to fill out questionnaires in a Mallorca airport, Spain

A few quick words about airport security, which is on everyone's mind these days. Security standards differ from country to country. Emotional people and rodent-lovers, in particular, take note.

X Rat Check
sign in Taiwan airport

Please stand on your turn.
For the safety of the passenger
it is prohibited to carry the dangerous things
in their hand bags of passenger.
❋ The hand bag
❋ Dangerous things as gasses and passions
sign in Kabul International Airport,
Afghanistan

Lodging

A fine hotel in a foreign land should be a wonderful "home away from home." It's a place to relax after hectic days of sightseeing or business, a place to reenergize and regroup. As such, it is wise to select a hotel that meets your specific needs. This should be no problem whatsoever. There is a wide range of hotels designed for different types of tourists, from go-getters to . . . well . . . let's just say, other types of travelers.

Hotel de Bastard
Lectoure, France

Aggressive Hotels
hotel chain, Cambodia

City Hotel &
Nut Club
sign on hotel, Japan

Because of the myriad of choices, you'll find hotel companies bending over backward to assure you, the English-speaking visitor, that their hotel is the right one for you.

Be prepared for a nerve-racking experience.
An outrageous rip-off on food and drinks
and hotel rates.
Lexus Clan hotel ad, The Manila
Bulletin, *Philippines*

bath in room, pavements in cooked
travel pamphlet, Sicily

We Serve you with Hostiality.
*from the Fu Hua and East Lake Hotels,
Guangdong, China*

Who among us can fail to be excited by such claims?

Always inquire beforehand about special rates or promotional programs. Room rates may include breakfast . . . or other things.

> Special Room Rats in August
>> *flyer from the Man Po Boutique Hotel,*
>> *Shanghai*

There is, however, a good chance you'll decide to pay less and forgo any special "extras."

> European Plan
> Measles not included in Room Charge
>> *hotel rate card, Seoul*

Regardless of the hotel you choose, you will almost certainly be touched by the efforts of the helpful staff to communicate in your own tongue. Signs, brochures, pamphlets—these are all designed to make you feel right at home, almost as if you hadn't left the States at all.

> The manager has personally passed all the water served here.
>> *sign in a hotel, Acapulco*

> Invisible service is available for your rest being not disturbed.
>> *notice in Yuanfei Hotel, Weifang, China*

Harold Tribune is available at lobby paper rack.
> *handout to guests at the Airport Garden*
> *Hotel, Seeduwa, Sri Lanka*

To get the best service possible, it is wise to make the right first impression. Abide by the management's requests you'll see posted in the lobby. These are usually extremely straightforward.

Good appearance please. No
watermelon please.
> *sign in lobby of Fragrant*
> *Hills Hotel, Beijing*

At the Cashier's counter kindly note that personal cheese are not accepted.
> *helpful hint included in Imperial Samui Hotel*
> *guidebook, Thailand*

No entries in upper clothes
> *Distik Hotel, Bishkek, Kyrgyzstan*

Not to perambulate the corridors in the hours of repose in the boots of ascension.
> *sign in ski hotel, Austria*

Guests are prohibited from walking around in the lobby in large groups in the nude.
> *sign in hotel lobby, Havana*

Some hotels are rather *liberal* when it comes to rules . . .

> Because of the impropriety of entertaining guests
> of the opposite sex in the bedroom, it is sug-
> gested that the lobby be used for this purpose.
>   *sign in hotel, Zurich*

Now it's onto the elevator and up to your room . . .
perhaps.

> To move the [elevator] cabin, push button of the
> wishing floor. If the cabin should enter more
> persons, each one should press the number of
> wishing floor. Driving is then going alphabeti-
> cally by natural order. Button retaining pressed
> position shows received command for visiting
> station.
>   *hotel elevator directions, Madrid*

> The lift is being fixed for the next day. During
> that time we regret that you will be unbearable.
>   *sign in hotel lobby, Bucharest, Romania*

Your hotel room will have all the amenities you expect . . . and some you won't.

> SHOWER CATCOME
> NEEDLE WOKE DAG
>   *items provided in the Wesun Hotel,*
>   *Wuhan, China*

Plus a plethora of extremely helpful hints for getting as comfortable as possible.

> Cooles and Heates: If you want just condition of warm in your room, please control yourself.
>> *from an information booklet about hotel air conditioner, Japan*

> If you wish, you may open the window.
> Do not open the Window.
>> *sign on window, Westin Chosun Hotel, Seoul*

> To speak to a guest in another room: Please follow these instructions: 1st Floor—add 250 to the room number and dial, on the 2nd, 3rd, and 4th Floors—dial the number required. 5th Floor—subtract 250 from the room number and dial, e.g. to contact Room 510 dial 260 EXCEPT for Room 542 whose number is 294.
>> *telephone instructions, Zimbabwe Sun Hotel*

> Please maintain temperature at 1 degree from 25, any higher or lower will only make the room hotter or colder.
>> *sign, Taipan Hotel, Bangkok*

No in the room
sign in Sri Racha resort, Thailand

Some rooms come with special features (or should we say "featules"?).

auto rock
lock on hotel door, Japan

Others, special services.

Please dial 7 to retrieve your auto from the garbage.
instructions on hotel-room phone, Rome

Take a second to look at emergency instructions (usually posted on your room door). You'll know just what to do if the worst happens.

When emergency, cover your mouse with your handkerchief.
sign in hotel, Japan

No smoking in bed. If it's on fire the guests should be disperse according to the safety way.
sign in room, Andingmen Hotel, Beijing

You might want to take a few minutes to refresh yourself after your plane trip. Pop into your bathroom and turn up the volume!

Volume On. Squelch. Please dial to shut whenever you want to.

labels above faucets in hotel bathroom, Japan

Voltage is 220 V but the use of the electric i rous or telt les is not permitted.

hotel brochure, Yugoslavia

Is forbitten to steal hotel towels please. If you are not person to do such thing is please not to read notis.

sign in hotel, Tokyo

You'll find that standards of cleanliness are often *remarkably* thorough.

Toilet was Cleaned and Spayed.

sign in hotel, Hue, Vietnam

And the complimentary toiletries are often *quite* enthusiastic!

The toothbrush is an indispensible part of enjoying life. I brush my teeth every day. I have a wonderful time. I like my toothbrush. I was won't to get up early.

wrapper on complimentary hotel toothbrush, Japan

Gives you strong mouth and refreshing wind!
claim on hotel toothpaste wrapper, Japan

You might want to take advantage of the hotel laundry service. These tend to be extremely versatile. You might be pleasantly surprised at the variety of items they'll clean—and so quickly too!

LAUNDRY BAG
19: Skirt
20: Stocking
21: Hand Kerchief
22: Big Towel
23: Small Towel
24: Hat
25: Shoes
26: Tie
27: Price of Ironing
28: Car with 12 to 15 seats
29: Car with 4 seats

laundry-bag list from Cam Do Hotel, Dalat, Vietnam

The flattening of underwear with plessure is the job of the chambermaid. Turn to her straight away.

in hotel brochure, Brno, Czech Republic

Feel free to use the hotel's or resort's recreational facilities, gift shops, or restaurants. You will note many exciting suggestions in the literature at the concierge's desk, or posted in common areas.

> For schedube and programmes of theaters as well as the tickets for all the types of performances, please, consult (he hall parter).
>
> *hotel brochure, Yugoslavia*

> Take one of our horse-driven city tours—we guarantee no miscarriages.
>
> *sign at in-hotel tourist agency, Czech Republic*

Hotel pools are a wonderful treat and something you'll surely want to enjoy. Just remember that safety is de rigueur!

> No Diving.
> No Nakedness.
> No Ruining.
>
> *sign at hotel pool, Istanbul*

> SWIMMING POOL SUGGESTIONS
> Open 24 hours. Lifeguard on duty 8AM to 8PM
> Drowning absolutely prohibited.
>
> *sign at Plantation Bay Resort, Philippines*

> Swimming is forbidden in the absence of the savior.
>
> *sign by hotel swimming pool, France*

Some hotels even offer more specialized swimming or bathing facilities (especially a plus for aviculturists).

Third Floor: Turkey Bath
> *sign at Hotel Palace, Seoul*

And you'll often find truly fine dining in the hotel itself. We guarantee that you won't be able to skip those meals!

Compulsory Buffet Breakfast
> *sign at Melia Hanoi Hotel, Vietnam*

A La Crate Menu
> *menu in the Pool Terrace (Over Looking the Sea), Sri Lanka Lavinia Hotel*

Tasty Tacos and Beautiful Tarts are the order of the day.
> *from promotional letter for guests of the Caravelle Hotel, Ho Chi Minh City, Vietnam*

A quick word about monetary matters: Some hotels prefer payment up front, others weekly; others have somewhat different time frames in mind.

Please settle your account at the coshier's weckly.
> *hotel brochure, Yugoslavia*

All rooms not denounced by twelve o'clock will
be paid for twicely.

sign in hotel, Budapest

What about storing your own money or valuables? The
hotel safe is always an option, but there are others as well.

Please deposit your valuables in the management.

room card, Guangdong Victory Hotel, China

The hotel is responsible for money valuables
only when deposited in the sofe at the reception
desk.

hotel brochure, Yugoslavia

Keep in mind: Hotels can be quite *adamant* about what
they consider unthoughtful guests.

Caution: Only you are responsible for your crim-
inal offence. The management.

hotel-door sign, Dhaka, Bangladesh

Please tell the public not to kill themselves on
hotel property if they want to die. It only con-
founds us. They can do it in the river for example.

*assistant public relations manager of the
Jakarta Hilton after a death at the hotel,
reported in* The Jakarta Post

As such, go by these general admonitions. Rather run-of-the-mill, perhaps, but they bear repeating.

> Please note that letting fireworks off in hotel guest-rooms is strictly prohibited.
>
> *sign in Hyatt Regency Macau, China*

> ✳ Visitor should be not carried: Arm, pets of material should be fired into the hotel.
> ✳ Visitor should be not ironed—cooked—washed. Hotel has got every service for a visitor.
>
> *posted hotel rules, Vietnam*

> Depositing the room key into another person is prohibited.
>
> *hotel sign, Japan*

> Do not hang wet clothes on lump shades.
>
> *hotel sign, Japan*

And gentlemen, take note:

> Foreigners are requested not to pull cock in Japanese bath.
>
> *ski-resort lodge, Japan*

As for honeymooners, well, let's put it this way: Why not the morning?

Guests must not come in their rooms after 11pm.
hotel brochure, China

One final note: Always remember that the hotel staff is there to serve you—in the *best* possible way, as the following example reminds us:

If there is anything we can do to assist and help you, please do not contact us.
letter to guests at Howard Plaza Hotel, Taipei, Taiwan

Sightseeing

The true joy of traveling, of course, comes from the unexpected, the unusual. Back home, you read your travel brochures with excitement. Now it's time to experience the authentic customs and pastimes of another culture. Yes, people are the same the world over. But sometimes they seem a little less the same . . .

At night the flavour changes as Turkish women don't tend to come out at night. Their absence has probably got something to do with the awful organ music that seems so popular here. It takes little persuasion for another tone deaf Turk to leap up in a lokanta and wildly pump his organ, singing incomprehensible words in between gasps for air.

from a Turkish travel article

Now that you're here, why not make a quick visit to a local travel agency and get the inside "dope" on the country and the sights you might want to see? Local agencies are more than happy to arrange side trips and tours. You'll marvel at the welcome you'll get.

Go Away.
sign in a Barcelona travel-agency window

And, of course, there are specialized agencies for every type of traveler.

Panicker's Travel, (reg'd)
sign in Agra, India

Lhasa Reception Centre For the Unorganized Tourists
sign in Tibet

Tourist Informants Upstairs (9 AM–5 PM)
sign, Japan

Some with names that conjure up pleasant visions of tourism past . . .

TITANIC Tours & Travel
travel agency in Udaipur, India

And others that clearly adhere to "truth in advertising" principles.

Asian Lines Co., Ltd.
We Pretend to Offer the Cheapest Fares
ad for Bangkok travel company

There also are specialized tours and hotel suggestions— such as this one, perhaps perfect for the "hearty eater."

Hi, I'm Manny, I recommend Varadero
Incl. 7 breakfasts & 3 dinners daily.
ad in Hong Kong

Take a minute to read the fascinating, tantalizing descriptions of the various side trips you can take.

If we are lucky we will see duck boys bringing their ducks home, men massaging their cocks on the road, cow boys taking grass. Yes it is a wonderful experience.
Tunas Indonesia Tours & Travel brochure

You'll also find suggestions for places to visit and things to do in pamphlets and glossy brochures—printed especially to whet the appetite of you, the intrepid tourist.

Would you like to ride on your own ass?
for donkey rides, Thailand

Stroll around our mahogany plantation. Scramble over stony tracks to nearby villages, or take a jeepney ride to the rapist monastery.
from travel brochure for the island province of Guimaras, Philippines

Untouched nautre chock o'block with upscale Amazon shopping malls, luxurious jungle-enclosed gated communities next door to the lowest extremes of underdevelopment, five-star boat cruises offering tourists Disneyland-like tribal dances inspired by the remains of native cultures.
ad for Amazon tour group, Brazil

In France, you can cruise on many canals and see the peculiarities.
brochure, French Canal Cruises

After a dawn visit to Borobudur, guests can choose to return atop a Sumatran female.
from Aman News, an Asian resort-group publication—referring to a female elephant

You'll learn of some opportunities that are literally impossible to enjoy back home!

Enjoy A Comfortable Stay in the Hills,
Comfortable Rooms Over Looking
"Adamspeak" Holy Mountain . . .
Also Enjoy the Sunset in the Morning
> *from ad for River View Watsala Inn,*
> *Sri Lanka*

Government officials often weigh in with "fun" suggestions of their own . . .

[Being taken hostage is] an adventure for the
tourist, because the tourist will end up learning
about the customs of the tribes as well as their
good hospitality.
> *speaker of Yemeni Parliament Abdullah*
> *Ahmar, on the practice of taking foreign*
> *visitors hostage*

Take part in activities of sex in rural sector.
> *brochure, Centre for Rural Development,*
> *National Economics University, Hanoi*

. . . not to mention happy insights into their people.

Even if the people in Haiti don't eat, they smile.
> *Michael Ange Voltaire, Haitian tourism*
> *official*

The Only Catholic Country in Asia! BEWARE
OF PICKPOCKETS
> *government-posted sign at Philippines tourist*
> *spot*

And they'll give you their own personal wishes for your
trip to their country.

It is our firm belief that your visit and stay here
will be worthwhile and forgetable.
> *letter from mayor of Dalian, China, inviting*
> *potential guests*

ZOOS AND
NATIONAL PARKS

Zoos and national parks are always exciting places to visit.
The enthusiasm of the staff can be most infectious.

BEIJING ZOO
Pandas and other miserable animals in cages
> *from ad in* Beijing This Month *magazine*

Budding naturalists will learn interesting facts about in-
digenous species.

Edible
Fur Can Be Used
Evil Animal
> *notices on animal cages, Shanghai Zoo*

Of course, don't feed the animals.

> Please do not feed the animals. If you have any
> suitable food, give it to the guard on duty.
>> *sign at Budapest zoo*

Or, for that matter . . .

> Don't Eat The Animals
>> *sign at Phuket Zoo, Thailand*

> Do not open your face to monkeys.
>> *sign, Nikko, Japan*

Should your visit be marred by problems—even of the pachyderm variety—rest assured that zoos and parks are prepared to help you.

> Elephant Complaints Here
>> *sign near Amber Fort, Jaipur, India*

> Tiger   Lion   First Aid
>> *sign at zoo, Rangoon, Burma*

As always, we urge you to follow the rules.

> Notice: Ramganga River is inhabited by croco-
> diles. Swimming is prohibited. Survivors will be
> prosecuted.
>> *sign, Corbett National Park, Uttar Pradesh,*
>> *India*

No picnicking, no botanizing and no uproaring in these gardens.

sign at botanical garden, Nikko, Japan

It is strictly forbidden on our black forest camping site that people of different sex, for instance, men and women, live together in one tent unless they are married with each other for that purpose.

sign posted in Germany's Black Forest

THEN IS STRICTLY FORBIDDEN TO:
a) Reserve box parking, spaces with chairs, fences, rape or other means.
b) Dainage of the plants and equiman
c) Not teak paper other box
d) Dig simples around tents
e) Play with ball of tamboury in the camp
g) Set to go into the camp, not autorized from the direction

from rules posted at Camping Atlanta,
Lungomare Sud, Italy

Please Bring a Pet's Excrement Home.

sign in park, Japan

MUSEUMS AND
HISTORIC SITES

Museums and historic sites can be fascinating for insights into local culture. Don't just look at the exhibits—*read* and *learn*!

> Brittany, Irland and Whales are almost connected, and still are today.
>> *helpful educational posting in museum,*
>> *Normandy*

> The painting, Wheatfield with Crows, probably painted before Van Gogh committed suicide.
>> *caption under photo of van Gogh's famous*
>> *painting, Malaysia*

> Paco Park and Cemetery during the Spanish era was very much alive with dead people.
>> *Philippines travel brochure*

> 2nd Floor Upstairs
>> *visitors' sign at historic convent, Philippines*

You might be lucky enough to visit the local equivalent of Colonial Williamsburg, where you can obtain an in-depth knowledge of arts and crafts.

> It is one of the most intensly cultivated forms of art in the city. In woodcraving, the treatment of the in-

tense plasticism converges with the condensement
of the notion of volume developed by the artisans,
imprinting an irresistable dynamic that submits the
statuary, predominating the despotism of framing
and the luxurious beauty of ornmentation.

> *from Air Azores in-flight travel magazine,*
> *Portugal*

Some of the local arts and crafts are ones you've un-
doubtedly always wondered about.

Local Fork Crafts Museum
> *on map, Furukawa, Japan*

Some sites, of course, make special requests of their
visitors.

Foot Wearing Prohibited
> *sign at Buddhist temple, Burma*

MATTERSTO
BE NOTED
DONT CAKVE DR MRITE
ANYTHING ONTHE GREAT
MALLDONT EKIT OR
LITTER NOSMOKING IN
THE AREA GO AHEARD ON
THE RIGHT SIDE DONT
STAND ON THE LEDGE
> *sign on the Great Wall, China*

OTHER SITES

Be sure to not overschedule yourself. Don't be tied to an itinerary, lest you be forced to bypass a roadside billboard beckoning you to a truly "foreign" experience.

> Mutianyu pablic pface ofent ertainment of erouts tonacle.
>> *tourist sign on fish farm, Mutianyu, China*

> Baltic Beer Fest! Come sample beers from several countries. Featuring both qualified and inebriated juries.
>> *in visitors' welcome magazine in St. Petersburg hotel*

You might want to check out other very special seasonal events.

> IT'S SUMMER TIME! Bring your children to the Garma Specialty Clinic for Circumcision. (Children and Adult). PAINLESS. BLOODLESS. GERMAN CUT.
>> *newspaper ad, Manila*

REST ROOMS, OR
"WHEN THE NEED STRIKES"

A quick note about public "facilities": We've all needed "to go" at one time or another—quickly, when we're not in our hotel room or place of business. What should the savvy traveler do?

First of all, scope out public rest rooms *before* you need them. Identifying them can be a bit tricky at times.

LAVATOLY
> *sign outside Hikone train station, Japan*
> *(unfortunately, the sign has since been*
> *corrected)*

Pubic Toilet
> *sign, Chinese railway station*

Be aware that the crucial distinction between men's and women's rooms can be a little blurred, if you will.

TOILET
GENTS
(LADIES ALSO)

> *sign, Bangkok*

Other times, though, the distinction is evident, if not quite *usual.*

Miss Toilet Left. Mister Toilet Down.
sign in Barcelona café

Genitl Emen
rest room sign, China

Men's
Refreshment Room
sign on men's room, Bangladesh

Toilet customs or attitudes may be . . . different.

Please Stop the Cock Uptight!
on urinal, Japan

Enjoy Stand
Toilet
sign in Chinese park

And bathroom-safety rules ones you're unaccustomed to.

Pls. fall in line outside to avoid suffocation.
Thank you for your cooperation.
sign outside public toilet, Philippines

But cleanliness is still a byword.

Tidy HO!
sign in ladies' room, Tokyo

Out of odor.
*sign on bathroom door, Taipei, Taiwan,
nightclub*

And for those of you who need some special assistance relating to rest rooms, may we suggest the following product (just use it with a bit of caution):

Atomic Enema
product name, Hong Kong

Culture and
the Arts

Ahh, culture! If you're a somewhat high-toned traveler, a trip overseas gives you a chance to sample
from a panoply of exciting and diverse cultural offerings,
the likes of which, we guarantee, you never will have run
across before. From peculiarly *intimate* musical perfor-
mances . . .

Russian Pianist Gives Exciting Rectal to Appre-
ciative Audience
    newspaper story, Athens

. . . to multitalented musicians . . .

We are going to present a Piano Recital by the Italian Cellist Mario Brunello
> *announcement by Pan Asia Concerts,*
> *Hong Kong*

From smarter Shakespeare . . .

Taming of the Shrewd
> *announcement at Radisson-Slavjanskaya*
> *Hotel, Moscow*

. . . to a more sensual Beethoven . . .

Art Theater: Birthday Concert; Beethoven's Symphony No. 3 in E flat maj. op. 55 "Erotica"
> *listing in* Mainichi Daily News, *Japan*

From Stephen King–style art and music . . .

LVNLTATLON
Mr. Cao Yong requests the horrour of your Presence at the Inouguration of the Painting Exhibition of himself. Beijing Artist Gallery.
> *invitation to art-gallery opening, Beijing*

There will be a Moscow Exhibition of Arts by 15,000 Soviet Republic painters and sculptors. These were executed over the past two years.
> *from* Soviet Weekly

Reach out and hold your mother's heart
slogan for the Seoul Children's Symphony

. . . to that touch of home away from home . . .

Good and old American music will be playing the park all the time. It's a festival that you can find full of "sneakers" feeling there.
in the entertainment-listings section of
Japanese magazine

And may we suggest a night at the opera? Remember, even if your French is a little rusty, you can easily follow along just by reading your helpful, English-friendly program.

Act One: Carmen, a cigarmakeress from a tobago factory loves Don Hose of the mounting guard. Carmen takes a flower from her corsets and lances it to Don Jose. . . . There was a noise inside the tobago factory and revolting cigarmakeresses bust onto the stage. Carmen is arrested and Don Jose is ordered to mounting guard on her but she subduces him and lets her escape.

Act Two: The tavern. Carmen sings . . . Enter two smugglers ("Ho, we have a mind in business.") Enter Escamillo, a Balls fighter. Carmen refuses to penetrate because Don Jose has liberated her from prison. He just now arrives. (Aria: "Slop here who comes.") But here are the bugles singing his retreat. Don Jose will leave and draws his sword. Called by Carmen's shrieks the two smugglers interfere with her. Jose is bound to dessert.

Act Three: A rocky landscape. Smugglers chatter. Carmen sees her death in the cards. Don Jose makes a date with her for the next Balls fight.

Act Four: A place in Seville. Procession of Ballfighters. The roaring of balls is heard in the arena. Escamillo enters (Aria and chorus: "Toreador, Toreador. All hail the Balls of a toreador.") Enter Don Jose. (Aria: "I besmooch you.") Carmen repels him. She wants to join with Escamillo now chaired by the crowd. Don Jose stabbs her. (Aria: "Oh, rupture, rupture.")

> *English program translation for the Genoa Opera Company's production of Bizet's* Carmen, *Italy*

FILM

Hollywood may be the international film capital, but when it comes to making exciting, meaningful movies, the rest of the world is no slouch either. So while on your trip, take an hour or two and go to a foreign film, or rent a video or DVD and get an insider's feel for the culture of the country you're visiting.

The range of foreign films can be tantalizing—and so exciting.

Egg! Egg?
    Swedish film (1975)

Recharge Grandmothers Exactly!
    Czechoslovakian film (1984)

I Go Oh No
    Taiwanese film (1984)

Who Created the YoYo? Who Created the Moon Buggy?
    Philippine film (1980)

Who indeed! And just like back home, hard-hitting advertising will draw you in—whether you like it or not.

Sabotage: An extremely enjoyable film for young and old that will shake your bottoms.
    advertisement for an Indian film

How Stella Got Her Guaranteed Seats
    sign on movie-theater marquee in Manila—
    advertising How Stella Got Her Groove
    Back—*and its seating arrangement*

Oldies fans may find fascinating filmic revivals from the past.

Chairman Mao Reviews the Mighty Contingent of the Cultural Revolution for the Fifth and Sixth Times
Chinese film (1967)

So settle down and enjoy the show! For those of us without the right language skills, helpful English-language subtitles will get us right into the action.

English subtitles from Hong Kong kung fu movies:

I'm not Jesus Christ, I'm Bunny.

Who gave you the nerve to be killed here?

Greetings, large black person. Let us not forget to form a team up together and go into the country to inflict the pain of our karate feets on some ass of the giant lizard person.

I am damn unsatisfied to be killed in this way.

Fatty, you with your thick face have hurt my instep.

You always use violence. I should've ordered glutinous rice chicken.

I'll fire aimlessly if you don't come out!

Beat him out of recognizable shape!

I got knife scars more than the number of your leg's hair!

I threat you! I challenge you meet me on the roof tonight for a duet!

I am sure you will not mind that I remove your manhoods and leave them out on the dessert flour for your aunts to eat.

Yah-hah, evil spider woman! I have captured you by the short rabbits and can now deliver you violently to your gynecologist for a thorough extermination.

Many visitors will want to watch U.S. films as well. Can't find it on the big screen? No problem! Just go to a local video or DVD store. They're ubiquitous nowadays, although sometimes you may have to look twice to realize you're near one.

Lental Video
video-store sign, Japan

And products may be a bit different as well . . .

DVD Lens Creaner
product sold at Japanese video store

Not Yet Old-Fashioned
> *blank VHS cassette label, Japan*

Service might even seem a trifle . . . abrupt.

ʹ Neo Nazi Service
> *name of video store in Nonthaburi (suburb of
> Bangkok), Thailand*

While you're shopping for your DVD or video, you'll want to read the liner notes—and see how truly well our films are understood abroad.

> *Alien II*: He repairs cottages and plants flowers. His eagerness to do good makes him one of the most popular.

> *The Swarm*: Monsters by the millions, and they are all for real! Excel to take the director of the disaster condition the text, once the successfully be responsible for the Neptunian number and skyscraper conflagration of a the action in the drama part, and have to feel the elephant of the public soul with result, have the authentic fact conduct and actions the basis, persons the details that match wits also there is certain science can't he stunt of the letter, high also increased then that penetrate everywhere.
> > *DVD liner notes, Taiwan*

Well, maybe things are a little different overseas after all!
But then, everything is, even TV. As the ad says:

Korea: four seasons, four senses
    ad for a Korean television station

And we have five of them back home! But no matter.
They appreciate us just the same. In fact, foreign film in-
dustries still look to Hollywood for inspiration. Indeed,
Hollywood has near-iconic status abroad. You'll find the
same Hollywood references, the same big stars, and you'll
hear the same immortal lines . . .

I found myself recalling the words of Marlon
Brando in On the Waterfront, "I could have
been a bartender."
    from an article in Look Japan, *Tokyo*

MUSIC

Music is truly the international language. So why not stop
into a music shop while you're overseas and sample some
new sounds? We bet you'll find it hard to leave!

Can't Stop! Music!
    *store sign in Takashimaya mall, Yokohama,
    Japan*

Hard Off
audio store, Japan

You may find some familiar, or at least *vaguely* familiar, names.

Jazz Recordings by jazz legend "Moles Davis"
Russian CD

Eric Crapton
Japanese CD

And others that aren't quite so familiar.

Bump of Chicken

Vlidge

Blankey Jet City

Dog Hairdressers

Supper Butter Dog

Mr. Children
names of Japanese pop bands

And still others that are somewhat *evocative*.

The Pees

Sound Masturbation

Bathtub Shitters

Flying Testicles

HIDE with Spread Beaver
names of Japanese pop bands

And our personal favorite:

Congenital Haemmhoroids
Japanese pop band

Read the liner notes to get fascinating insights into these foreign artists.

Do we have boyfriends? We are interested in delicious food and sweets. And tiny animals like the cat.
Naoko Yamano, of Japanese rock band
Shonen Knife

And scan some song lyrics.

I want to throw my brain of a half,
I want to throw my brain of a half,
wanna throw it away.
from "Brain," sung by Japanese
pop band the Pees

I and love don't kiss me noisy
love don't kiss me only
> *from "Kissin' Noise," by top*
> *Japanese pop band Glay*

He's the groove, he's the man, that new Pope in the Vatican.
> *from a 1979 Italian disco chart-topper about*
> *Pope John Paul II*

We venture to guess you'll run across catchy songs you've never heard before—and may never want to hear again.

"I Still Love You Even Though You Are a Married Man"
"All Girls Want That"
"Kill Me With an Injection Please" [about a woman who is in love with a doctor]
> *hit songs banned by the Cambodian*
> *government for "cheapening Cambodian*
> *women," according to Minister of Women's*
> *and Veterans' Affairs Mu Sochua*

"I'm Vasectomized"
> *song that reached number three on Thai charts*
> *in the early 1980s*

And don't miss the "golden oldies" section for some jumpin' commie faves!

"Care Shown for a Company's Hot House"
"Let's Sing This Glory of Having the Respected
    Leader"
"The Day When I Received the Distinguished
    Service Medal"
"Mixed Duet Sounds Over the Fields of Rich
    Harvest"
"The Song of the 10-Point Political Program"
"Robot is Introduced into my Working Place"
    *North Korean songs, performed by the North
    Korean Army Ensemble*

"Indignantly Condemn the Wang-Chan-Chiang-
    Yao Gang of Four"
    hit song of 1976, according to People's Daily,
    Beijing

"Mother, I want to Go to the Mountainside and
    Harden Myself with Physical Labor"
"Last Night I Dreamed of Chairman Mao"
    Communist Chinese hit songs

And if you're nostalgic for some good old American or
Brit pop, you can find that too. Just like home!

It is wonderful to be here
it is certainly a thrill
you are such a lovely audience

we would like to take you home with us
we would rub to take you home
> lyrics to "Sergeant Pepper's Lonely Hearts
> Club Band," as printed on Japanese pachinko-
> parlor advertisement

I see trees of greed redes too I see there bleem for me and you and I think to myself "What a wonderful world."
> lyrics to "What a Wonderful World," as
> printed in Korea

Dylan's Bob Greatest Hits
> audiocassette sold in Saudi Arabia

Chris Isaak: vacals, guitar
Kenny Dale Jonnson: drums, vacals
Rowland Salley: bass, vacals
Jimmy Pugh: Hermmond B3
Johnny Reno: sex, vocals
> pirate copy jacket info on Chris Isaak CD
> Forever Blue, sold in Hanoi

Remember what the doorman said/
Keep your hat! Keep your hat!
> lyrics to Jefferson Airplane's "White Rabbit,"
> as sung by Japanese '60s band the Mops

Fans can even get their favorite rock star T-shirts!

Who the Fuck is Mick Jagger?
printed on T-shirt, Japan

Yes, music truly is a wonderful form of clear communication among different peoples around the world.

Its life could be one of these cheap folhetins, of that if they turn pages and are shot in the next garbage can. Which what!!
Brazilian CD liner notes

Which what indeed!

Sports and Games

And now a brief word for the sports lover—or that more sedentary game player: Your overseas trip is no time to stop playing!

You'll find top-rated clubs waiting for you . . .

Green Feel Golf Club
golf resort, Kochi, Japan

. . . with pros waiting to give you their interesting "inside tips."

Why the Right Dimples on Your Balls Can Help
headline, The Nation, *Bangkok*

Specialized stores cater to even the most eclectic of sports enthusiasts.

SPORTS AND HOBBITS
sign in bookstore, Taiwan

And you may find even more specialized sporting magazines, especially for cyclists, who certainly seem to do more than just ride.

Mr. Bike: Magazine for windy people
Japanese magazine

In speed record attempts, the cyclist pedals just a few meters behind a car that breaks wind for the rider.
item about a Dutch cyclist in the South China Morning Post

Local sports coverage is often quite good, and makes you realize that sports interviews are just as intelligent and insightful abroad as they are back home.

This coach is crazy. He can't ask me to run like this. He must think I have two lungs.
player from the Brazilian soccer team Rio Claro, complaining to a TV reporter

Reporter [in German]: How long has your team been training?

> U.S. handball team coach Javier Cuesta [in En-
> glish]: We've been together since January,
> training five days a week, four to five hours a
> day.
> Translator [taking microphone and also speaking
> English]: We've been together since January,
> training five days a week, four to five hours a
> day.
>> *during a press conference after a U.S.-*
>> *Germany handball match in Germany*

Then again, some sports coverage (not to mention the sports covered) is a trifle different.

> Penalties for cheating in potato-growing contests
> are among the severest in the civilized world.
>> *in the* Gaberone Star, *Botswana*

Lucky travelers might arrive during one of the many international game series. One thing is for certain: They're not like the World Series.

> The Southeast Asian Games is the Arena in Ma-
> nuring the Sense of Solidarity Among the Na-
> tions of the Region.
>> *banner, Jakarta*

Can't speak the local lingo? No problem; at most international athletic competitions, helpful translations are provided for the English speaker.

At none European championship in athletic there were so many people from TV at one place as it will be in Split.

Many honorable people will be at Poljud during the European championship in athletic. Sports and political. Juan Antonio Samaranch, MOK president, ambassadors from many countries the highest Yugoslav functioners.

You may put, if you want, part of the representative in a hotel. "Split", in the new built part. Some representatives will come in Split in the number less expected. . . . Our representatives will mostly arrive on the European championship one by one maybe in groups, but not complete.

> *press information, European Athletics*
> *Championships, Split, Croatia*

Besides sports, you'll probably discover a whole range of exciting new games to play. This one is so easy to learn, you'll want to begin right away!

Temporarily each of you, four players, represent a side and the very same man picks up the dice and throws once so as to see who is going to represent the temporary east and so on. If the number of points are 3, 7, 11 the man opposite the East, the West, if 2, 6, 10 the man on the right or the

South, if 4, 8, 12, the man on the left, the North, and if 5, or 9 the East himself starts drawing the topmost Position Indicator, the second, third and fourth by the south, west and north in their respective order and turn (counter clockwise). In turning over the Indicator each one of you will find where you are to be seated. By this simple process, the allotment of seats is determined.

instructions on seating players included in mah-jongg game, China

And then, of course, there's the Carrot Game. (Need we say more?)

Carrot Game
Official Supply
Song of the Carrot Game
Digging carrots, muddy & muddy
Washing them, cut & cut
The soup boiling well, hot & hot
we all favorite carrot game

game label, Japan

Visiting Embassies Overseas

An unexpected "perk" of your trip abroad may be an invitation to a glittering embassy party. Quite often the U.S. ambassador or consul general will invite fellow Americans from all walks of life for cocktails and a chance to meet local dignitaries.

Are these dull and stuffy affairs? Far from it! You can't begin to imagine what diplomats do when they let their hair down.

> The wedding was consummated in the garden of the American Consul's home in the presence of more than a hundred distinguished guests.
>   The Japan Times

What a wonderful opportunity to watch our diplomats (and theirs) exchange pleasantries—ever so sensitive to the nuances of language . . .

> Chinese host, lifting his glass in a toast to his American guests: Up your bottoms.
> American diplomat: Up yours too.
> > *overheard at cocktail party boasting numerous international guests in Shenyang, China*

> I am not wanting to make too long speech tonight as I am knowing your old English saying, "Early to bed and up with the cock."
> > *Hungarian diplomat, in speech at embassy party*

You may meet local luminaries, such as friends of our defense attaché (typically very colorful, battle-hardened characters).

> The pilot of the fighter, identified as Captain Kim Yong-bae, was reported to have ejaculated shortly before the crash to safety and was evacuated to a nearby military hospital.
> > Korea Times

Or perhaps religious leaders, enthusiastically showing off their "human" side . . .

I will now open these trousers, and reveal some even more precious treasures to Your Royal Highness.

> *archbishop of Uppsala, Sweden, trying to impress an English royal visitor with his knowledge of English*

Always you'll find conversation far-ranging and *most* intriguing . . .

Dorothy Macmillan: What are you looking forward to now?

Madame de Gaulle: A penis.

(shocked silence)

General de Gaulle: My dear, I think the English don't pronounce the word quite like that. It's not "a penis" but " 'appiness."

> *exchange at a French dinner party at the time of General de Gaulle's retirement*

Equal goes it loose.

> *former German president Heinrich Lubke, translating* Gleich geht es los (*"It will soon begin"*) *into English*

You may even get to meet one of our intrepid foreign correspondents, always savvy regarding local customs. (Travelers' Tip: They're a wonderful source of insider knowledge.)

Reporter (in front of Russian sign): Are you having any trouble with the Russian language?

Newscaster Connie Chung: Not at all.

Reporter: Well, then, why are you standing in the men's room?

Getting Around:
Public Transportation

Ah, that first exciting day getting out and about and exploring. Public transportation might be your best bet, particularly because in some places walking around town can be . . . difficult.

Please Walk Backwards
> *Public Works Department sign on street in*
> *Singapore*

So shall we take a cab? A bus? A train? In general, we don't recommend buses. Bus routes are usually limited, and the schedules can be tricky.

Please note that the adjustment of the schedule of Route No. A35 (Mui-Wo-Airport) which will take effect from Wednesday, 1 March 2000, will be postponed for a month.

> *sign posted by New Lantau Bus Company, Hong Kong*

Bus stops may not be as welcoming as you'd like.

Shitseeing Bus Stop
> *listing on tourist information map, Japan*

Waiting Will Be Prosecuted
> *sign on street, Japan*

And bus-line names can be a bit difficult to keep on the tip of your tongue.

YNAPMOC ELIBOMOTUA LEVART NAM-MUY
> *bus-line name as translated into English and painted on the side of the bus, under the Chinese characters (unfortunately, the painters printed it from right to left, just as the Chinese characters were)*

In addition, bus rules aren't always easy to follow.

Keep all fours in bus—eyes only out window.
> *sign in Mexican bus*

London Buses
Let's Enjoy Yourselves
sign on Japanese double-decker bus

By contrast, taxicabs give you the freedom to roam the city and countryside at will. You will have to be attentive to be sure you're charged the correct fare. Cabs typically carry helpful instructions in English to ensure this.

1. This meter taxi already anti-meter to time.
2. If the tariff flashing light should be standby.
instructions printed inside Jakarta taxicabs

They also often include helpful reminders.

Don't forget to carry your thing.
sign posted in Shanghai taxi

Passengers are not allowed to carry with them contraband goods, smoke, spit or to dump inside taxis. Psychos or drunkards without guardians are prohibited to take taxis.
rules posted in Shanghai taxi

Please fasten seatbelt to prepare for crash.
sign in taxi, Shibuya, Japan

And taxi commissions can be quite concerned about making sure you're having the best time possible—in *all* aspects of your trip.

> Intercourse Discomfort Report Center
> *posted in taxi, Seoul*

Trains are another commonly used tourist conveyance. Who can resist this stirring call to "ride the rails"?

> Train
> + Ing
> Traing

> *advertising slogan for East Japan Railway*
> *Company—posted throughout stations and*
> *famous among English-speaking visitors who*
> *can't figure out what it's supposed to mean*

Look for very special fares.

> Discunt Ticket
> *sign in Japanese train station*

Signs in railway stations and trains will regale you with the most interesting information.

> Strong winds caused by train
> *sign at Todaimae Station, Japan*

Water not potatoble.
> *sign on Italian train*

Coffee on Rolls
> *name of coffee carts in Bahnhof Zoo railway*
> *station, Berlin*

For rest rooms, go back toward your behind.
> *sign, Japanese Railways station*

Ask the station employee about a trouble.
> *sign in railroad station, Japan*

Ferries and boats offer an entirely different travel experience. Why not take, for example, an exotic river trip?

Far up the river your journey is through mostly primary forest with impenetrable, undergrowth, Giant Orchids, Mangrove flowers, hugetress with puthon crapping for branches, tropical bulfrongs . . .
> *Kalimantan, Indonesia, travel-agency*
> *brochure*

Just remember to be a neat—and serious—tourist!

Sanitary Bog:
Useful for containing
various dregs and dust.
> *Hong Kong ferry bag*

ENGINE ROOM IS SERIOUS PLACE
sign on door in hydrofoil, Yangtze River, China

Then again, upon reading certain signs, perhaps you'll want to rethink that watery trip.

Adults: 1 USD
Child: 50 cents
Cadavers: subject to negotiation
sign at ferry terminal, Davao, Philippines

DO NOT LEAN ON THE WIDOW

sign on Mediterranean cruise ship

In all cases, when traveling by water, do take the time to read all handily posted notices, which *may* help you in the event of an emergency.

Helpsavering apparata in emergings behold many whistles! Associate the stringing apparata about the bosoms and meet behind. Flee then to the indifferent lifesaving shippen obediencing the instructs of the vessel chef.
emergency instructions on Russian ship in the Black Sea

Getting Around: Driving

One of the best ways to truly get the "lay of the land" when you're in another country is to rent a car and explore the highways and byways on your own. You'll find local car-rental agencies most helpful and extremely interested in pursuing a rather *intimate* working relationship with you.

> We are really hopping this will be the first step of a long and successful copulation.
>> *confirmation letter from Kanungsuk car-rental*
>> *service, Bangkok*

If you want to feel the wind in your face, you may opt for other, perhaps unique, modes of transportation.

> Motto-Circle for Rant
> *sign in Angkor Tom Hotel, Siem Reap,*
> *Cambodia*

Or you might want to try motor scooters, available in a wide variety of models. In addition to the usual features, these often come with slogans painted on them. Let the world know what kind of a scooter cyclist you are! Just pick the one that suits you best and zoom away.

> Urban Trend: It reaches for the sky. Neither does civilization.

> Man-boy: You'll enjoy it.

> Fuzzy Scooter

> Jog 50: The friendliest scooter on Earth.

> Curio: The ultimate scooter.

> Movie 125: Your future depends on it.

> Cabin: With fashionable feeling.

> Party 100: Flying angel of elegant, nimble, and beautiful.

Dio: Shuttle in the city jengle, The new, speedy snail clan.

Hold Me: Enjoy the lovely satisfaction on the road.

> *scooter brands (and the slogans printed on them), Taiwan*

But most of us prefer a car when traveling in foreign countries. You'll find those big brand-name car-rental companies wherever you are.

Bomb
Car Rental

> *name of car-rental company, Chiang Mai, Thailand*

Don't be surprised, however, if you can't rent a good old American Ford Taurus—or even a good old Japanese Toyota Camry. No, you'll probably be offered other exciting, new, and, er, unusual choices. Decisions, decisions! Should you rent a

Mitsubishi Mini Active Urban Sandal
Subaru Gravel Express
Mazda Bongo Friendlee
Daihatsu Town Cube

> *Japanese automobiles displayed at a 1996 Tokyo trade show, reproduced here as they appeared in English on each vehicle*

Or would you be more comfortable in a

> Nissan Prairie Joy
> Mitsubishi Debonair Exceed
> Suzuki Every Joy Pop Turbo
> Mitsubishi Delica Space Gear Cruising Active
> Mazda Proceed Marvie
> Subaru Sambar Dias Astonish!!
>> *Japanese automobile names displayed at 1996*
>> *Tokyo trade show, as they appeared in English*
>> *on each vehicle*

And if you're planning some off-road adventuring, may we suggest:

> Daihatsu Rugger Field Sports Resin Top
> Isuzu Mysterious Utility Wizard
> Nissan Big Thumb Harmonized Truck
> Mazda Scrum
> Mitsubishi Libero RVR Super Wild Gear
> Isuzu Giga 20 Light Dump
>> *Japanese SUV and light truck names displayed*
>> *at 1996 Tokyo trade show, as they appeared in*
>> *English on each vehicle*

Families may opt for the Every Joy Pop Turbo, which comes equipped with a family-friendly slogan painted right on the side:

Everyone has different personality and taste. If they get together, it makes a family. 'Every' is always staying near our life.

on Mitsubishi microvan, Japan

Once you've rented your car, the rental agency will usually provide you with a manual offering helpful hints and fascinating insider driving tips.

To stop the vehicle, release the accelerator pedal and apply the brakes.

Volvo manual

If you crash, you can be injured.

Honda CRX manual

The fuel level gauge indicates the quantity of fuel in the tank.

foreign sports-car manual

They might even throw in a packet of easy-to-follow local rules of the road.

1. At the rise of the hand of the policeman, stop rapidly. Do not pass him or otherwise disrespect him.

2. If pedestrian obstacle your path, tootle horn melodiously. If he continue to obstacle, tootle horn vigorously and utter vocal warning such "Hi, Hi."

3. If wandering horse by roadside obstacle your path, beware that he do not take fright as you pass him. Go soothingly by, or stop by roadside till he pass away.

4. If road mope obstacle your path, refrain from pass on hill or round curve. Follow patiently till road arrive at straight level stretch. Then tootle horn melodiously and step on, passing at left and waving hand courteously to honorable road mope in passing.

5. Beware of greasy corner where lurk skid demon. Cease step on, approach slowly, round cautiously, resume step on gradually.

from official Japanese guide for English-speaking drivers

Drivers of power-driven vehicles who commit any of the following violations are liable to a fin up to five yuan or a warning:

1. Stopping at the pedestrian crossing

Article 40, Road Rules, Beijing

In case of any accident the hirer must immediately report to our Shep.

car-rental contract, Chiang Mai, Thailand

Of course, if you're planning a long-term visit, you might simply want to buy a car. Overseas, they often come with extras unavailable in the States.

Car and owner for sale.
>   *sign on car, Manila*

Now it's time to hit the road! Make sure you obey all traffic signs and signals, even if they're not quite what you're used to seeing at home.

Stop: Drive Sideways.
>   *detour sign, Kyushu, Japan*

Try Bigger and Bigger but keep More and More Slowly.
>   *traffic sign, Tokyo*

Cars will not have Intercourse on this Bridge.
>   *traffic sign, Tokyo*

Traffic may be conges to subjection.
>   *road sign, Hong Kong*

Drive Carefully.
Your lovers are waiting for you.
>   *billboard, Philippines*

Go Slow.
Someone is Wetting for You.
>   *highway sign, India*

Be on the alert for road-hazard warnings. (Remember, you're not on I-95 anymore!) The signs, however, are usually self-explanatory.

BEWARE OF FALLING CARPENTERS
at construction site, Manila

DANGER:
SLOW MEN AT WORK
Brunei

Danger Ahead
Fasten Safety Belts
And Remove Dentures
Namibia

Caution
Water on Road During Rain
Malaysia

But sometimes not.

SEQENTIACCY EXC
URSION PRITHEEN
OT CALL FOR CEO
WDED ADVERENCE
Jiangsu, China

Sometimes they're more than a little enigmatic.

The Slippery Are Very Crafty
*Chinese road sign literally translated to the
English, which is supposed to mean "Caution:
Wet Roads"*

Beware of safety.
    Suzhou, China

Obey all local parking regulations to the letter of the law
(even if some of the letters are missing . . .)

Temporary Parking Pot.
Parking Within Line. Stop Befor
Step Down. Leave After Step In.
    parking sign, Xiamen, China

(. . . or added . . .)

Do not use parking lot as we expect a great deal
of dustle.
    in notice sent by the Immigration Office,
    Tokyo

(. . . or simply baffling).

Park one hour. Later Dick Dock goes the money
clock.
    sign posted in shopping district, Athens

ParkinginwrongPlaces Will Makeyou accountal-
betoLaw Apartfrom being atresPassingontheRight
oftheCitizenandthestate
    parking sign, Luxor, Egypt

If you run into car trouble, stop at a local gas station or car-repair shop. (You may have to look twice to be exactly sure where you're stopping.)

Cat Oven
sign, car-repair shop, Bali

You'll probably find the service most attentive . . .

Feel you Up?
sign, Japanese gas station

And the products, super!

Superglans
Netherlands car wax

Super Piss
Finnish solvent to unfreeze car locks

Then you're back on the road again . . . maybe.

No More.
Please Pack Up Now.
road sign at dead end, Istanbul

Shopping

Now for a little shopping—a wonderful way to soak up local color and snap up a few souvenirs. Wherever you are, you will find local merchants eager to sell you, the happy tourist, a wide variety of goods.

We have no good things to sell.
sign on shop, Lovina Beach, Bali

You Want It, We Had It.
sign at Japanese electronics shop

Sorry—We're Open
sign outside Istanbul carpet shop

Who knows what you'll find . . .

STUFF ONLY
sign on door, PC World, Kyoto, Japan

Copulation Accessories
sign, China

. . . at intriguing, exotic stores like . . .

Kaka's
Penang, Malaysia

Yellow Dick
Okinawa, Japan

Hot Dog
pet store, Busan, Korea

Beaver Reform Showroom
Japan

Hair by Fabric
Yokohama, Japan

Even the shopping bags are intriguing!

I hope the best to all like dream.
>   *logo on bag, Blagoveshchensk, Russia*

I'm a Foot Soldier.
No Human! Go Ape!!
>   *slogan on store's canvas tote bag, Japan*

Now baby. Tonight I am feeling cool and hard boiled.
>   *slogan on Japanese shopping bag*

London XYZ. All those floodlights spin your head around. Dance and prance across the stage shaking things in a peculiar way.
>   *slogan on Japanese shopping bag*

HAPPY SWAN strewing the "Sky" Sand—that brings happiness, a white swan flies. To that city? Or to what city will she fly.
>   *slogan on Japanese shopping bag*

Sneep Dip
>   *slogan on Japanese shopping bag*

Some shopping bags even come with helpful hints.

I am a bag
>   *on tote bag, Japan*

Warning: This is not a tin.
    bag from Tianjin, China

One thing is for certain: You're not at the local mall back home. No, stores and shopping overseas can be quite different, perhaps a little more exuberantly . . . ursine, shall we say?

CIAO PANIC is where you can walk and spin around with bearfoot, and scream at the top of my lungs and no one cares.
    poster advertising a shop, Japan

Granted, some stores, though, are a little less than exuberant.

We try our best to decrease your life
    advertising slogan on store, China

But most stores simply let it all hang out.

Hung Long
    store in Vietnam

S&M Shopping Arcade
    shopping center, Japan

Key Fuctory
    store sign, Japan

Ten Fuk Store
store in Shanghai

Wanko
store in Hong Kong

Of course, for all that wide variety of stores, you can't necessarily expect to find the perfect gift. In fact, you may find certain stores will "go the extra mile" and even tell you how little to expect.

68% Perfect Shop
shop name, Medan, Indonesia

You might be stunned by their honesty.

At a Fiction of the Original Cost
ad, Malaysia Furniture Center

Rest assured, though, throughout your shopping day you will be overwhelmed by their "customer-friendly" attitude.

Get out of the way or you'll get killed.
Are you buying or not? Have you made up your
    mind?
Buy if you can afford it, otherwise get out of here!
If you're not buying, don't ask.
If you want it, speak up; if you don't, get out of
    the way.

Don't talk so much. Say it quickly.
Didn't you hear me? What do you have ears for?
Stop shouting! Can't you see I'm eating?
Don't you see I'm busy? What's the hurry?
I can't solve this. Go complain to whoever you
     want.
Why didn't you choose well when you bought it.
The price is posted. Can't you see it yourself?
> *commonly used phrases by Chinese retail-store*
> *clerks, banned by the Chinese government in*
> *1995 as part of its national politeness*
> *campaign*

And you'll be impressed by their "English-friendly" service.

English well talking. Here speeching American.
> *sign in shop, Mallorca, Spain*

English smoken.
> *sign in shop window, Marrakesh*

But don't be taken in by the first store you see. Savvy shoppers the world over know if you paid full price, you weren't shopping smart. Be on the lookout for surprising offers.

Up From Half Price!
> *sign in Hong Kong store*

SALE This shop challenging to price broken in
this campaign sale.
> *sign in Japanese store*

And clearance sales the likes of which you've probably
never dreamed.

ANAL Clearance
> *sign in Hong Kong store, was supposed to read
> "Final" (the F and I were squeezed together to
> fit in the window . . . becoming an A)*

Not to mention unique "gift with purchase" deals.

Upon presenting this ad with a US $50 purchase.
You will receive our complimentary gift package
consisting of: 3 hand embroidered handker-
chiefs, 2 hand embroidered guests towels and one
embroidered hot roll.
> *ad in the* Curaçao Gazette

The array of products you'll find in stores is vast. Smart
shoppers should always be on the lookout for top foreign brands of electronics and appliances, household
name brands you'd be proud to show your friends back
home.

Smeg
> *refrigerator brand, Italy*

CRUDE
Fancy and Convenient Kitchen Accessories
ad for Crude-brand appliances, Tokyo

Hornyphon
Austrian video recorder

Assman
German tape recorder

These products often offer unique extras you won't find
on domestic models.

Hitachi.
Your personal life.
Every day it bring fresh wind.
television label, Japan

Not to mention ironclad guarantees.

Guaranteed to work throughout its useful life.
claim on box of Hong Kong–made toy

Fortunately for the English speaker, these items usually
come equipped with helpful instructions in English.

Omron Photo cell; Quote: if apperatus tend to
fail, be sure to clean mucky from lens.
instructions with Chinese camera

Very close to translamissing station you may find useful to put the high low sensitivity to low.
instructions on German radio

When the Basic Time corresponds to the pre-set Alarm Time, the alarm is generated. The alarm tune will automatically cease after 1 minute working. If you have a depress on "SNOOZE" while it is alarmed, the loud will stop immediately and loud for another 8 minutes after having this "SNOOZE" 8 minutes and so on. . . . However, alarm will not effect if it has lasted for fully 8 minutes unless the second correspondence that is to say after 24 hours.
instructions for Chinese travel alarm clock

You'll even read general advice—adages to repeat and remember:

Please use quality batties. Don't use bad batties.
instructions for electrical appliance, Japan

For many travelers, of course, the real joy of overseas shopping comes from buying vintage treasures, exquisitely crafted items from times gone by. Avid collectors will spend many joyful hours hunting down and buying that genuine, "one-of-a-kind" antique.

Chinese historical relic All reproduced with Unique Traditional Graftsmanship
ad, Hong Kong

K. T. Berata Antiques. Made to Order.
> *sign, Bali*

Others may opt for traditional crafts—items made with love, care, craftsmanship . . . and sobriety.

> When the value of luxury become
> Purity and sobriety are the highest expression
> Big leather pieces only joint by an intangible
>   stitching balance
> You will enjoy exact volumes and shapes blend-
>   ing into
>> *ad for furniture store, Italy*

Others of you may track down special somethings you simply can't find elsewhere.

> THE MUTUAL CARESS TORSION CUSHION.
> This is a magic little item that, once yours, will fan your zest for love into a blaze, allowing you to do anything your heart desires. It restores the energy of youth, and the rage!
>> *Chinese product*

> Human-biting Mosquito Trap
>> *product, Singapore*

And finally, others may want to purchase wonderful examples of traditional calligraphy, expressing even more wonderful thoughts—for that special "someone" back home.

May every memory bring the feeling that you have not lived for anything.

>   *translation enclosed with piece of Chinese*
>   *calligraphy for tourists, Hong Kong*

Shopping for Clothing and Accessories

It's always fun to stroll around the fashion district, do a little window shopping, and pick up some of the latest styles to wow your friends back home. Almost wherever you go, you'll find a tantalizing mixture of haute couture and trendy streetwear at some of the world's smartest boutiques.

Sexy Cramp
Wearhouse
clothing store, Japan

UGLYGIRL boutique
clothing store, Beijing

Violence Jack Off
clothing store, Japan

ZEUS
Queen of Modernity
clothing store, Japan

Fashion Communication Biscuit
clothing store, Japan

Horse Shit
casual clothing store, Japan

Store signs and window advertisements will draw you in.

Dresses for street walking.
sign outside Paris dress shop

Yo! Casual Street Freeks
Are Suck enough so
just get out of there!
ad in store window, Shibuya, Japan

Be on the lookout for brand names you know—at a *fraction* of the cost!

Harley-Dabeson
The Gret

American
Fredom
Machin
on back of jacket, Japan

Kate Spayed New York
logo on handbag, Thailand

Sports fans, rejoice! You'll even find great deals on your favorite team shirts.

The Green Bay Peckers
T-shirt, Japan

Philadelphia Sexers
T-shirt, Japan

And, trend spotters, keep an eye out for next year's hot designer names!

Down And Out
handbag brand, Germany

Trim Pecker trousers
Fancy Pimple jeans
brand names, Japan

Flip through the racks and you might just find that perfect outfit to make you feel sleek, chic, and ever so glamourous.

Drug Store Body. Let's get the Good Shape and have a sexy body just like a pig.

slogan on Japanese overalls

You never know what you'll find in these exotic shops—even specialized hosiery!

Super Soft
Computerized
Socks

socks label, Madras, India

Cherilon Pantyhose: To Help Prevent Tried Legs

panty-hose slogan, Thailand

Ladies Pile
Soft and Worm

tag on women's socks, Japan

Sabrina—We introduce you the "Zokki Support System"; SABRINA. She'll be one of your closest friends, and this one will last. Slip on. You feel it. Watch out when you step out without SABRINA.

from panty-hose package, Japan

You'll also find jewelry and accessories. Traveler's tip: If you fall in love with that gorgeous pair of pierced earrings, don't worry if your ears aren't pierced. Just get it done at the local jewelers, where the procedure will be . . . quick.

We make holes in ears with gun
store sign, Mussoorie, India

You'll also find, of course, that ubiquitous American uniform—the T-shirt—but with a foreign twist. Many of these are emblazoned with catchy slogans *in English*—front and back—making them ideal gifts for folks back home. There's something for everyone, T-shirts with slogans perfect for *every* type of person.

From the med student or doctor . . .

FATALISM
We may have overlooked
Irritable bowel syndrome is two to three times
more common
on Japanese sweatshirt

. . . to your teenage relatives . . .

Melon Boy I am so glad that we met let's try to
become close friends.
T-shirt slogan, China

. . . to those with what might be called a philosophical bent . . .

WHO WILL BELL THE CAT?
T-shirt slogan, Japan

What kind of world is this?
It's kind of crap!
> *T-shirt slogan, Japan*

. . . to those budding political activists . . .

Save the apartheid boycott of the lesbian Nazi lettuce growers for Jesus of the nuclear whale.
> *slogan on T-shirt, Bangkok (it sold out in one day)*

I trusted the government, now my dick glows in the dark
> *slogan on T-shirt seen on young woman, Bangkok*

. . . to the free-spirited . . .

Kinky Orgy
> *T-shirt slogan, Japan*

And, of course, something for everyone in between!

Child be a public servant. The best balance of music and technology within a vaguely.
> *T-shirt slogan, Hong Kong*

Bizarre
MUST

Awesome
WANT
  T-shirt slogan, Japan

Flying Bunny
Follow me if you come
  T-shirt slogan, Japan

Use prppose on inner fearny of sotiofoction to you
  T-shirt slogan, Japan

HIPPIES MADE TOO KEEP ASSHOLES
  T-shirt slogan, Japan

We have considered the point of contact between body and cities. Between his motion and
her personal appearance and between the tide of
time and the wave of life.
  T-shirt slogan, Japan

I'M COCK
I'm home. I'm all alone. I need some hot coffee.
There were three jovial Welshman . . .
  part of slogan, Japanese sweatshirt

Those of you from colder climes can pick up jackets with
slogans that make equally thoughtful gifts.

Bitter & Stupid
  logo on jackets popular in Shinjuku, Japan

Come Flesh
> *slogan on jacket worn by an elderly woman,*
> *Japan*

When you're shopping, be sure to read the care labels on the items you're thinking of buying. You may be surprised at what you'll learn.

LABEL
Beware of Limitations!
This genuine Rip Curl garment was built for your comfort and pleasure. Have fun and keep Surfing.
> *label in counterfeit garment—knocking off an*
> *American item—in Indonesia*

WILL PIPS ORIGINAL WEAR
The design which it made the most of the good point of the material for to the full
> *slogan on Japanese clothing brand*

Our clothes make healthy and sexy impression to us. It transforms you completely and giving you happy times.
> *clothing label, Japan*

A few brief words especially for the men: Who needs Brooks Brothers when you can shop at . . .

Men's Biggi
> *menswear shop, Tokyo*

You'll find sophisticated, cosmopolitan style for today's man!

Mecca of Dude, Dundy, or Fop
menswear-shop sign, Tokyo

BASIC AND EXCITING
Refreshed and foppish sense and comfortable and flesh styles will catch you who belong to city-groups
on label of men's sweater, Japan

There are usually great tailors who can stitch you up a custom suit for an unbeatable price. (Just be sure to get that name right!)

Ufixnahsnahs
name of tailor shop in Hunan, China (the man's name is actually Shan Shan Xi Fu)

As for off-the-rack sportswear, seek out clothing with that extra something (shall we call it seasoning?):

Mac Donel
Pure Clothes
Daily Wear
Greatest Taste
Real Flavor
label, men's shirt, Japan

Southbreeze Authentic Jeans
Natural Taste
slogan on denim shirt, Japan

You can always stock up on the "essentials" . . . with that little extra something as well. (Shall we call it . . . well, let's not go there!)

MEN'S UNDER WEAR
We'll advise you about your "stickiness" about your daily life.
on men's underwear tag, Japan

SWORD UNDERWEAR:
✸ Extra comfort
✸ More absorbent
✸ Extra strength
✸ Longer wear
✸ Meat resistant
label on men's underwear, Southeast Asia

HANG-IT-OUT COTTON BRIEFS
The brief you can trust
ad for men's underwear, Philippines

And for those with "different" orientations, may we suggest . . .

Pansy men's underwear
underwear brand, China

And for those who *are* just "different" . . .

> Mighty Oak: I only have one or two of something.
>> *slogan on underwear, Japan*

While we're on the topic of underwear, let us note that the ladies too can find remarkable twists on the old panty standby:

> Cassia: Ladie's Portable Panties
>> *women's underwear brand, China*

> Cop Lingerie
>> *lingerie store, Taiwan*

> Woody Home
>> *women's underwear brand, Japan*

> WEARUNDERS
> Now feel the thrill of Paris under your spine.
> French Wearunders.
>> *ad for French underwear licensed to Bhilwara,*
>> *India*

After a hard day of shopping, why not stop at a nearby shoe store . . .

> Pee Shoes
>> *shoe store, India*

. . . and pick up a new pair of comfortable shoes.

Makes walking tiring
slogan on shoes, Jakarta

Shoes to make your street-walking more relaxed.
ad slogan, Tokyo, Japan

You won't even have to worry about the right fit!

THIS SHOES IS BEST FITTING
written on top of a pair of shoes, Japan

Pampering Yourself: Visiting Beauty Shops and Spas

Overseas spas can offer you wonderful beauty-enhancing and relaxation-inducing treatments. So pamper yourself and step into one of these inviting, exciting salons!

Poop
beauty shop, Aichi, Japan

Oily Beauty Centre
beauty salon, Hong Kong

Beauty Brain's Fantastic Fannie
beauty salon, Japan

And adventurous male tourists may want to try these bar-bershops:

> Slasher barber and massage center
> *Philippines*

> Hair Cook Pit
> *Japan*

The expertise is often of the "Highest" caliber.

> God Hands
> Hair Shop
> (since 1988)
> *hair salon, Japan*

Surely the new treatments offered will entice you to spend a little extra money.

TUKAR BEAUTY SALON
Specializes in Pimple Sucking
> *sign in Pattaya, Thailand*

CHERRY BEAUTY TREATMENT CENTER
Facial, slimming . . . male removal.
> *ad in Sarawak, Borneo*

Finger Cutting Saloon
> *section of beauty parlor, Goa, India*

Why not drop a few dollars on exclusive cosmetics as well? Who needs Chanel or Clinique when there's . . .

Fanity Fancl
cosmetics line, Japan

Tense Up cosmetics
Fancl House cosmetics line, Hong Kong

Sini 5.5 Lotion
(Senile group)
label on Chinese moisturizer

ACNE
facial cleanser, Japan

And don't pass up the wonderful hair-grooming products.

Go Gay shampoo
Yugoslavia

Geraid
for men
Design Mud
Claim the wild & beautiful
Can't stand being just like other guy
Make your skin & hair beautiful
men's grooming product, Japan

Geraid
for Men
Hair Wild Slime
> *men's hair-grooming product, Japan*

NUDY
HAIR WATER MILK
> *hairstyling product, Japan*

For the comming of the fortunate moment.
CHANGE ABOUT ME. IT'S JOY JACK.
> *men's hair tonic, Japan*

Oily Shampoo
> *shampoo, Japan*

Use repeatedly for severe damage
> *on shampoo bottle, Japan*

Massage is a wonderful way to work away the kinks from a hard day of sightseeing. (Just go early.)

Massage and Lulur: Tired Masseuse
Please Call LIA 3182222 ID 67905
> *ad, Jakarta*

Why, a relaxing massage may even get you primed for a hot night on the town—or reduce that need altogether.

TRADITIONAL JAVANESE MASSAGE
A full body massage with genital and moderate pressure

> *in brochure of very exclusive Majapahit City Club, Surabaya, Indonesia*

You'll find specialized massage services that promise very little . . .

Milky Way Massage Center: Reflexology; Best and natural way to enrich health and beauty without causing any effects.

> *sign in Bangkok*

. . . or maybe a little too much . . .

We unblock your constipation with our fingers.

> *ad, Al Sin Foot Reflexology Centre, Hong Kong*

And if you want to surprise the folks back home with a new, slimmer you, no need to weight!

Wait Reduction Programme

> *Premasiri Supermarket, Sri Lanka*

Some of the weight-loss treatments are quite innovative.

The application of this product can produce a prominent effect in decomposing and reducing the excess fat accumulated in the abdomen, the things and the butterock, as well as making the skin flat.

Slimming Bath Essence packet, China

More Slime Diet Food
food line, Tokyo

Dining Out

Never—ever!—confine yourself to eating at hotel restaurants. Why limit yourself when there are so many eateries offering so much in the way of tempting—and authentic—food at lower prices? And when, indeed, the exotic names of the restaurants are so utterly *tantalizing* . . .

GREASY Fast Food Restaurant
Quezon City, Philippines

My Dung
Vietnam

Mr. Beef Seafood Restaurant
Beijing

Dead Fish
Siem Reap, Cambodia

Cafe de Cancer
Japan

Stomach Care Snack Bar
Ghana

Placebo Labor Handbag

Manual Birth Pet
Nagasaki, Japan

CAFE SCHWANZ
TAKEOUT OK
window sign in Tokyo coffee shop

And who among us can resist the proud boasts of these restaurateurs?

We don't serve dog, cat, rat or worm
restaurant sign, Siem Reap, Cambodia

The buffet, the likes of which can't be found anywhere, offers all the rat meat and other items you can eat.
sign at Binh Quoi Green Tourist Park, Ho Chi Minh City, Vietnam

We serve Pork with fresh garbage!
restaurant sign, Vietnam

Nightmare Italian Food
restaurant promotion, Jakarta

Candlelight dining with gourmet dishes that blend the sickness of Thai flavors to continental cuisine.
on menu of Lotus Noir restaurant, Thailand

We serve people like you as good food
restaurant sign, Japan

You have no reason to try our restaurant.
slogan of Le Cafe, Jakarta

Travelers, take note: Unlike in the States, restaurants in other countries may be quite exclusionary or, dare we say, discriminatory?

Seafood brought in by customers will not be entertained.
restaurant sign, Langkawi, Malaysia

Others welcome all types with open arms.

For those of our customers who are vegetables, we are able to offer a plate of hot mixed vegetables.
from Italian restaurant menu, La Patata, Tokyo

In addition, be aware that some restaurants may have dress codes that you may be unused to.

> A sports jacket may be worn to dinner, but no trousers.
>
> *on restaurant menu, France*

And, of course, a restaurant may ask you, the customer, to comply with its special "foreign" rules. Some may be a little . . . surprising.

> No eating and drinking.
>
> *sign in Satay King restaurant, Hong Kong*

Others, a tad obscure . . .

> NO! CARRY WITH!!
>
> *sign in Nakatsugawa, Japan, restaurant*

> PLEASE WAIT TO BE THE SEAT.
>
> *sign in restaurant, Hong Kong*

But, no matter what, you will always be greeted with open arms and genuine "across the seas" friendship.

> No talking to cashier. No smoking. No fighting. No credit.
> No outside food. No sitting long. No talking loud. No spitting.

No bargaining. No water to outsiders. No
     change. No telephone.
No match sticks. No discussing gambling. No
     newspaper. No combing. No beef. No leg on
     chair. No hard liquor allowed. No address
     enquiry.
          sign outside Bastani Cafe, Bombay

Now you take your table and happily scan the menu, ru-
minating over the myriad of delicious gustatory delights.
What will you eat tonight? It can indeed be difficult to decide when faced with such a range of exotic menu
choices.

     You will probably start with an appetizer . . .

Appendix salad (pork)
     menu item, Thailand

Tasteless Soup
     menu item, Savannakhet, Laos

SKEWERED STUFF
     *menu item, restaurant at Soraksan National
     Park, South Korea*

Chicken Mouse in Tartlet
     menu item, restaurant in Jakarta airport

Main dishes hold another set of adventures for the true
gourmet!

Spaghetti Boneless
    menu item, Kasthamandap Restaurant,
    Kathmandu, Nepal

Fried Uterus
    menu item, Hanoi

Fillet of Leather Jacket in a saffron cream sauce
and vegetables
    menu item, Grappa's Country Restaurant,
    Hong Kong

Shrimps in Spit
Bacon and Germs
    menu items, Tokyo

Meat lovers will find a wide selection of rather unusual, er,
mortal morsels . . .

Green people with beef fried rice
    menu item, Hsinchu, Taiwan

Roasted Banker and Cream Sauce
    menu item, Hiking Restaurant, Shanghai

Fried fishermen
    menu item, Japan

Muscles of Marines
    menu item, Egypt

Grilled Maitre d'Hotel
   menu item, Bali

Children Sandwiches
   menu item, Vienna

Tenderloin of Pork Merchant, Vegetables
   menu item, Thai Airways International

Lumb and ladies finger stew
   menu item listed in a Greek guidebook

Fried Vegetarians Wrapped in Egg White
   menu item, Jade City Restaurant, Zhuhai,
   China

Cold shredded children and sea blubber in spicy
sauce
   menu item at a Wanchai, China, restaurant

Toes with butter and jam
   menu item, Bali

Some meats even have proper names!

Fred frigid cuttle
Fred Snack Head with Five
   menu items, Hanoi

The truly sensuous gourmet may prefer these house specialties:

Thigh Lambskin
menu item, Moraira, Spain

Pork Condom Bleu
menu item, Vung Tau, Vietnam

Spaghetti with seamen sauce
menu item, Lake Garda, Italy

Ham on penis
menu item, Warsaw

More "down-to-earth" diners may want to try

Deep Fried Peking Dumplings
Peking Dumping in Soup
menu items, Wally Matt restaurant,
Hong Kong

Crap Roll
Crap Cream Spaghetti
Crap Cream Risotto
menu items, Italian restaurant, Seoul

Grilled Potties
menu item, Mexico

You might well want to sample old favorites with an interesting international twist . . .

Chocolate Clam Chowder
menu item, France

Gordon Blu
menu item, Moraira, Spain

Lobster Thermos
menu item, Cairo

Sir Loin steak with potato cheeps
menu item, Singapore

Or you could opt for what may be called truly "cutting-edge" cuisine . . .

Natural Fish Knife (piece)
menu item, Moraira, Spain

. . . and dishes you've never seen before:

Indonesian Nazi Goreng
menu item, At Village, Hong Kong restaurant

Utmost of chicken fried in bother
menu item, Macao

Buttered saucepans and fried hormones
menu item, Japan

Fried friendship
menu item, Nepal

For those who simply can't make up their mind, there's always

Fried Et Cetera
menu item, Tokyo

Traveler's Tip: Reading a foreign menu can be tricky, as distinctions among dishes are sometimes very subtle.

Roast Pig
Roast Pork
menu items, Hue, Vietnam

Boiled Tasteless Jam Pork Soup————10,000
Boiled Tasteless Jam Pork Soup————10,000
Boiled Tasteless Jam Pork Soup————10,000
Boiled Tasteless Jam Pork Soup————10,000
from Thippavongsay Restaurant, Laos

You'll marvel at how *fresh* the ingredients can be.

If you happen to find wounded wild birds or animals, please send them to the station, which is

located in Room 507, Large Roest Restaurant, 19
Beisanhuanzhonglu.
in newspaper listing, China

Of course, you will want to supplement your entrée with
several tasty side dishes. The waiter may suggest

Horse-rubbish sauce
menu item, Rome

Screw with Chinese Herbs

Fried Rice from Hell

Fried Convoluted Watch
menu items, Hanoi

What about drinks? Again, your options are many,
whether you want soda or juice.

Coca-Cola coke
Coca-Cola pepsi
menu items, Vietnam

Hot coke
menu item, Japan

Minced Pork Date Shake
menu item, China

Flesh Juice
menu item, Japan

Or something with a little more "kick."

Hard Riqur
menu item, Japan

Barking Beer
menu item, Savanakhet, Laos

Koff
Finnish beer

REEB
beer, Shanghai

We also advise you to scan the wine list to see what the sommelier recommends.

Our wines leave you nothing to hope for.
on menu of Swiss restaurant

Make your choice, then bottoms up!

Spanking Wine
menu item, Beijing

Cockbum Special Reserve Port
menu item, Hong Kong

One final tip: If you feel you aren't receiving the kind of service you think you deserve, speak up! Take a lead from high-ranking officials who aren't afraid to give the "down and dirty" details about poor service to the management:

> Sir, I have been fingering your waitress for a long time, but she just does not want to come.
> *Joseph "Erap" Estrada, then vice president of the Philippines, complaining to restaurant manager when a waitress ignored his gestures and failed to come over to the table*

Or take the sage advice written on a Cairo menu:

> If you are wishing to show your feelings, wait until you see the manageress.

Nightlife

It may be 9 P.M., but your day is hardly over! The bright lights of the nightclub scene beckon you. But why not have a drink in the hotel bar first?

Welcome to Piano lounge where you could enjoy abundant beverages besides cocktails in an elegant atmosphere while being introxicated.
Longman Hotel brochure, Shanghai

Hotel Bar. No drinking prohibited.
sign in cocktail lounge, Turkey

You may be "loose enough" now to shake your booty at the local disco.

OK 100 Dicos
disco, China

White House Disco is for people who thinks discoteque:
❋ is for wild young people with no taste for elegance
❋ is noisy. It's too cheap a place to visit with a boy friend.
❋ Services are poor and no high-class guests around. It's no place for me.
❋ Why, my time to have a bottle of whiskey kept must have expired!
from disco pamphlet, Japan

Let's fun.
disco ad, Luxembourg

Traveler's Tip: If you have Internet access, you might want to check local websites for information—even free passes—to area clubs. These sites often offer literally *unbelievable* help.

Great part of the palimpsest is classified to the young people, with programs speeches, mixed and championships from valid D.J., are also several musical classification. In the course of the

programs complimentary tickets come to the assigned times, in order to approach in the best discotheques of the zone.
Important!
If in the translation of our pages, they appear of the errors caused from the translator, we pray You of communicate to us

from "Radio Idea" website, Molfetta, Italy

Incidentally, if you're not a great dancer, not to worry.

One of the longest bars in Moscow meets you in the "Snowstorm" nightclub a floor above where over 800 sq. m. are at your disposal for tet-a-tet dinner or weird dancing

Snowstorm nightclub ad, Moscow

If you want to rub elbows with the "natives," try one of the local clubs. Be careful, though; some are *quite* exclusive.

Members and Non-Members Only
sign outside Mexico's Mandinga Disco

Nobody can come to the Medusa Business Club.
ad slogan, Ho Chi Minh City, Vietnam

And there are always those picturesque nearby bars and pubs . . .

Bar Anus Pub
> *Puerto de la Cruz, Canary Islands*

. . . some with quite unique amenities!

Jaya Pub. The Pub with a Difference. The only
Pub where you can bring your wife, girl friend &
mother in law. . . . . .AND STILL ENJOY!
> *ad, Jakarta*

FUJI KARAOKE
❊ The Best Private VIP Room on Kon Samui
❊ Top Service by Beautiful Hostages
> *sign in Ko Samui, Thailand*

Child Bear
> *sign on a Bihar, India, bar—trying to advertise*
> *the fact that they sell chilled beer*

Special cocktails for the ladies with nuts
> *sign in Tokyo bar*

no one really goes to
aqua bar for the drinks,
but we make sure our won't kill you.
this is something you must remember.
> *window sign, Aqua Bar, Japan*

CROSS BAR
So fuckin' guy get good thing,
But I don't know about it.

And sole good guy getbad thing
But I don't know about it.
What a hell's going on.
  bar sign, Japan

As for the last statement, we say, good question.

One thing to keep in mind during your pub crawl: The "rules of the road" may be a little different from what you're used to.

Ladies are requested not to have children at the bar.
  sign in cocktail lounge, Norway

No ladies in the bra—she's lounge only.
  sign in hotel, Milan

Please note that this café reserves the right not to entertain patrons who fall under the following three categories
1. Impatient Patrons
2. Long Sour FacePatrons
3. Loud Soft Speaking Patrons
  sign at Could-Not-Cope-Up Café, Kuala Lumpur, Malaysia

Wherever you go, *please* don't just order a plain old vodka tonic or scotch on the rocks. Try the local specialities of the house! In other words, when in Guizhou, do as the Guizhouans do, and order a

Pingba Jiaojiu: High smell harmonized with good smell, sweet after be drunk, with long smell
proud claim of Pingba Jiaojiu, alcoholic drink produced in Guizhou, China

You may find that even the old standbys taste a little different. The secret? Maybe it's the ingredients.

World's finest whiskey made from Scotland's finest grapes
for Japanese whiskey

Those unlucky in love might want to drown their sorrows in an appropriate Dutch speciality:

Fockink liqueur
liqueur brand, Netherlands

Or pop into an appropriate bar—maybe you'll get lucky!

Dick and Uprise
bar, Japan

And there are always "girlie clubs," even for the intellectual set . . .

Best Virgin with Sunset Paradigm
Tokyo nightclub

. . . not to mention those with foot fetishes!

GIRLS GIRLS GIRLS—Live Shoes Daily
    Hong Kong bar sign

Those of you who, instead, want male companionship in
your quest to "paint the town (or even your house) red,"
may want to try

ABBIE'S MALE
Young n' charming male masseuses
Councelling services for relationships
House Painting
For enquiries, pls call Sam
    flyer, Singapore

And for the really lonely, there's always your beer
pitcher . . .

Draft The Clean Beer
Beer produced newly
Beer comes in the mouth,
And love comes in at the eye,
    on Crown beer pitcher, Pusan, South Korea

. . . or your coaster.

I'm sexy. Admire Me. Touch Me. Taste Me. And
Take Me Home.
    *printed coaster, Holiday Inn, Colombo, Sri
    Lanka*

Police

Travelers abroad are prime targets for crime. It's an unfortunate reality of life. You must be vigilant at all times to avoid a wide variety of typical tourist-related crimes—muggings, hotel burglary, holdups, kidnappings, violent apes, purse snatchings, etc.

An extremely violent ape is roaming the town. Please avoid making eye contact.

police warning given out in Shimosuwa, Japan, after a male macaque scratched and bit more than 23 women

May we suggest you follow this very helpful—if somewhat general—"hint," courtesy of the Hong Kong government:

> Beware of People
> *sign posted in Hong Kong*

Should you find yourself a victim of a crime, do exactly
what the authorities in your host country tell you.

> If you have been the victim of a crime during
> your stay in Ecuador, please denounce it here.
> *sign on police station, Guayaquil airport,*
> *Ecuador*

You'll often find the police in very close proximity.

> What Trouble Will You Have? Please Call The
> Police Behind You.
> *sign, Thailand*

If possible, seek out those police officers who are specially
trained to deal with English-speaking tourists and, in fact,
assiduously study useful and strikingly realistic sample di-
alogues to better serve you, the tourist.

> Policeman: What countryman are you?
> Sailor: I am sailor belong to the Golden Eagle,
>   the British ship.
> Policeman: Why do you strike this jinriksha
>   man?

Sailor: He told me impolitely.

Policeman: What does he told you impolitely?

Sailor: He insulted me, saying loudly "the Sailor, the sailor" when I am passing here.

Policeman: Do you striking this man for that?

Sailor: Yes.

Policeman: But do not strike him for it is forbidded.

Sailor: I strike him no more.

from The Practical Use of (English) Conversation for Police Authorities, *Japan*

But what if the "worst" happens, and you find yourself unwittingly on the wrong side of the law? Be aware that you may face quite *large* penalties.

You did not report yourself by the Alien police. You have to do this in a short time, otherwise you get troubles! When you don't come to our office, we demand you to come! And when you don't come again, you maybe have to pay a fine, and it is possible that you will be expanded.

letter sent by Rotterdam, Netherlands, immigration police to someone who did not show up for registration appointment

It might be a good idea to seek out crack legal expertise. Find a top-notch attorney who has passed some of the more rigorous legal examinations:

2. (a) "Necessity knwows no law." Discus
5. What is hurt. Or culpasle homicide.
6. What is defarnation?
8 (a) A is at work with a batchet; the bead fires off and ills a man who is standing by. Has A committed any offence?

>*legal test questions at Bombay University, as reported in* The Times of India

Learning the Local Language

A phrase or two in the local lingo goes a long way. Your native hosts are "tickled pink" when you order food or bargain in their language. You'll notice the difference in how they treat you!

Myanmarpyi.com has prepared few Myanmar Language Lessons. People in Myanmar will show more hostility if you speak Myanmar words to Myanmar people.
    ad for Myanmar website

The U.S. State Department publishes a series of helpful books for the intrepid language learner. After a quick perusal of one of these guides—with easy-to-follow grammatical rules—you'll be speaking like a native in no time!

> In the case of the first possessive, the pattern is: *Basic form of the first possessive*, (or corresponding possessive form if modified by a possessive adjective in English) plus *dative of the third person "his" form of the second possessive* plus *definite article* plus *third person "his" form of word possessed*, to agree in number and case according to its form and use in the sentence.
>
> Hungarian: Basic Course, *publication of U.S. State Department*

On the other hand, maybe you'd rather pick up a foreign-language guide once you're there. They're packed with those helpful phrases you're certainly going to need over and over again.

> Bring me, we are in a harry!
> Bring me a partion of . . .
> Only a half a partion of . . .
> Smocking/No Smocking
> Greek flavourable sweets and candies
> Chocolates: plain, milk, Pavlidoo, bitter
> This is to go at deffered rate (halt rate)
> I cannot speek . . .
>
> *"Helpful words and phrases,"* in Learn Greek with Me *English-Greek Dictionary, Athens*

In truth, though, often you don't really need to learn the local language, since so many of our international friends are learning how to speak English correctly (if somewhat pedantically).

Using Your Brain to Read English
    English guide, Japan

Thinking Logically to Feel Confident about Reading English
    English guide, Japan

Or perhaps not so correctly . . .

Correctly English in 100 Days
    East Asian book for beginning English speakers

Good English In As Little Time
    Egyptian English-language primer

If books fail, there are always special language-arts schools where people can learn alien tongues—perhaps literally.

Outerspace Language School
    Ho Chi Minh City, Vietnam

So why not give the locals a chance to "test the English-language waters" by allowing them to converse with you in their brand of English?

AT THE FRUIT SHOP

"Hello, fruiterer! Have you some nice fruits here? How much for a bench of bananas?"

"Five hundreds rupiahs."

"The price is okay. Give me two benches please. Thank you. I hope I don't bore to come here again."

>*suggested conversation in book* English Conversations, *Indonesia*

AT THE SHOW SHOP

"Good morning. Have you Belly shoes?"

"What number do you want?"

>*suggested conversation in book* English Conversations, *Indonesia*

You may be surprised at how many familiar colloquialisms you'll hear.

To use an English phrase, he is a host in himself.

>*from* English-Chinese Word Ocean Dictionary

To craunch a marmoset.
Do you cut the hairs?
The stone as roll not heap up not foam.
Nothing some money, nothing of Swiss.

Exculpate me by your brother's.
She make the prude.
> *catchy English phrases to learn in* The New
> Guide of the Conversation in Portuguese
> and English

Or see . . .

Fack You Man
> *spray-painted graffiti, Japan*

And you'll find that people are the same the world over.
Now that they're speaking English, they're saying the very
same things you may hear in downtown Dayton!

You've mistaken that banana for a telephone!
> *handy English phrase, Japanese textbook*

I'm verry sorry I clogged the sink. I just didn't
want to vomit on the floor.
> *Sentence #12 in* Making Excuses in English,
> *Japan*

Is your girlfriend beautiful?
No, she is rather ugly.
I have sea sick.
Why do you escape from jail?
> English Conversations, *Indonesia*

Bad boy! You break wind very badly (with too
bad smell)
You ars quite sexy girl (laday)
Don't make goo-goo eyessat me.
Hey! you want to strip me, don't you?
A boy and a girl are lipping (lip against lip)
She opened her bossom for her lover.
She sat snugging her boy-friend.

> 3000 Khmer English Phrases, *Phnom Penh,*
> *Cambodia*

Fancy giving free education! This is a paradise
for the people, indeed!
His Excellency Kim Il Sung is the greatest genius
of the present times.
Here is a bumper crop. We have a bumper crop
every year.
Bookseller! Have you "Kim Il Sung Selected
Works" Vol 1, 2, 3, 4, 5, 6?

> *suggested catchy phrases to learn in the North
> Korean government book* Speak in Korean

—Hello! Mrs. Reed? This is Mr. Schmuck, from
the Global Encyclopedia Corporation.
—I'm not really very interestest in a new set of
encyclopedias, Mr. Schmuck.

> *"Learn English" column,* Korea Times

Writing Home

Don't forget to write the folks back home and tell them all about your trip! Stop into a stationery shop and buy an . . .

Air Mail Writhing Pad
on pad from Almaktaba Stores, Saudi Arabia

. . . or . . .

Campus Fecund
Japanese notebook paper

Some stationery products come "pre-equipped" with in-
spiring printed messages, things you'll surely want to
share with your loved ones.

Drifting story of a awkward bear and pretty pen-
guins. DON'T ABANDON HOPES, THERE IS
THE DENOUEMENT. Hey, here, here we are!!

This notebook having horizontal ruled line and
being able to fold up is the best for arranging sen-
tences

HAPPINESS We"re a purely couple and we believe each other so much
stationery, Japan

Beautiful Life: Teacups brimming with dreams
and hopes gork us all
slogan on Color Wave notepaper, South Korea

Sunny Garden
Be sticky about nature
I touched a tiny nature.
on address book and cashbook, Japan

CHERRY DREAM
We little cheery dream. Do you like? I am chee-
ful of cherry.
printed on Japanese stationery

Passage Open 9*14 SAT
HOOKED ON REGATTA AND INDULGING

IN MAHLER FOR FOUR YEARS IN TOXI-
CATED BY SHOOTING FOR THREE YEARS
KNOWNING ABOUT THE USELESSNESS
OF TALENT AND THE PLEASURE OF WORK
HAS MADE ME FOREGET THE FLOW OF
TIME. I FOUND MYSELF AFTER HAVING
BECOME AWARE OF WHAT VIOLENCE,
FREEDOM AND SUFFICIENCY WERE WE
CANNOT LIVE ON POWER ALONE. BUT I
DON'T WANT TO LIVE A DULL LIFE. I BE-
COME MYSELF IN A SUNNY PLACE. THAT
IS CALLED PASSAGE. IT IS ON THE HILL
PAST THROUGH THE PATHWAY IN YOUR
HEART PASSAGE.

envelope from accessories shop, Kobe, Japan

Sometimes the sentiments do the talking for you. And so you may wish to give these items as gifts to that "girl next door."

Happy Days of Young Sheep: I' 'm a sheep, young handsome sheep. They say every sheep looks like me very much. But look at them carefully. Their faces are a little bit difference. So I' 'm lonesome sheep. Would you date me?

on stationery, Japan

Traveler's Tip: Too busy to write a letter? Buy a postcard, the kind that comes complete with a little English-language sentiment accompanying a picture of a cute puppy or beautiful waterfall. Remember, a greeting card or postcard is a thoughtful, quick way of telling Mom and Dad, elderly uncles and aunts, "All is well, wish you were here."

> For you
> I always think of your thing
>> *Japanese greeting card*

> Pleasure Show
> She goes by her feaking
>> *postcard, Japan*

> European dogs
> European dogs are living freely.
> It is open and Elegantly.
> European cats
> Many cats are doing usual life
> In the beautiful scenery and the streets. We can see that one part.
>> *Japanese postcard*

> The grass is appear whiter than looking shining!!
>> *on Japanese postcard featuring two photos of a puppy*

Ready to mail your letter or card, but can't remember that special someone's address? Don't worry about it!

> Letter Box for Wrongly Addressed Letters
>> *sign on mailbox, Brunei*

Holidays and
Special Events

Many of you might be overseas for a special occasion—the holidays, a wedding—perhaps your *own* wedding. Whatever the cause for celebration, we'll bet you'll find *plenty* to make what you're doing a one-of-a-kind event!

Celebrating a birthday? No need to forgo the traditional birthday cake—with that special heartwarming message in frosting.

Happy Birthday 20 set dish and fork and one knife
> *as written in frosting on birthday cake, after tourist phoned American Pie Restaurant in Hong Kong*

And, of course, the traditional birthday card—also with that special heartwarming message.

FUNNY TOWN'S THEATER
STARRING FUNKY FANNY
> *birthday card, Japan*

Getting married? Services for weddings—or approximations thereof—are readily available.

Beautiful arrangements for you Wetting Event!
> *sign, Hong Kong florist*

Weeding Photos
> *cover of wedding album, Russia*

And if you want to look special on your perfect day—*both* of you . . .

We are doing bridal make up for gents and ladies.
> *ad,* The Statesman, *Calcutta*

You'll get a slew of wedding cards you'll surely want to paste in your scrapbook.

happy wedding
on your marriage
    Japanese greeting card

And if you want the honeymoon to continue (for at least a short time), check out overseas marriage counseling.

to enjoy married life 9AM to 1PM Ayurvedic
Centre New Delhi
    ad in Hindustan Times, *India*

Finally, should your marital (or should we say martial?) relations be "blessed" while you're still abroad, expect to receive the appropriate good wishes.

The slow measure of the chanted war song as soldier do, and bold and high
    congratulations-on-your-new-baby card,
    China

And now for holidays. Let's start with Christmas. Celebrating this holiday abroad is, indeed, an exceptional treat. You'll hear the strains of those familiar Christmas carols wafting through the air and . . . well, you know the words. Heck, why not sing along!

"Hark the Harold Angel"
    Christmas carol listed in Bangkok church
    bulletin

"I Saw Murray Kissing Santa Claus"
*Christmas-carol title on Kowloon school
handout, Hong Kong*

Hark the herald angels sign,
glory to the newborn King;
Peace on earth and mercy mild,
Gold and sinners reconciled.
from lyric sheet at Hong Kong church

Stores will often be decked out with those familiar holiday decorations and signs. Why, it's just like home!

Merry Chrastmas
sign in store window, Japan

Santa. I've been a good girl.
Please Stop.
*display sign held by a cartoon girl, on lap of
Santa mannequin, Japanese store*

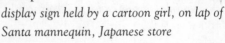

We wish you are merry Christmas
sign on store window, Japan

And, of course, you'll see displays of Christmas cards that truly convey your holiday wishes.

Let the birds singing for you freely.
Affectionated your heart with firendship.

Decorated your dreams with fresh flowers.
Merry christmas to you.
> *Christmas card, China*

If you wish hard enough, your Christmas dearms
really will come ture.
> *Christmas card, China*

Season's
gree
nd
Be   Wishi
ou
A
Hap
> *Christmas card, China*

Some Christmas cards ask that age-old question:

Merry Christmas!
Have you done a nice boy & girl?

> *Christmas card, Japan*

You can even pick up wonderful Christmas decorations
with intangible extras!

200 chasing light with muscing
> *on box of Christmas-tree lights, China*

Celebrating other holidays overseas is equally exciting and exotic.

> For turning tricks on Halloween
> *sign in costume shop, Hong Kong*

> Grow in Dark Witches with Dicks
> *on invoice for broomstick-riding Halloween
> witches, China*

You may find some holiday customs overseas a little different. But take the opportunity to enjoy another culture's way of celebrating.

> A Father's Day Offering
> Free Digital Rectal Examination
> *banner at Ministry of Health, Philippines*

In Case of Emergency

Should you find yourself in need of medical care while traveling, rest assured that the language barrier needn't pose a problem—particularly if you maintain a *flexible* linguistic attitude.

Before being treated, you should be prepared to answer a few simple questions about your condition. This handy list may help.

Are you haunted by horribles?
Do you ever run after your nose?
Does your nose choke?
Does your head or face or shoulder ever limp?

Has any part of your body suddenly grown un-
controllable?
Do you have heart thrills?
Do you have hot fit?
Do you feel as if there were two when there is
only one?
Are more than half your teeth off?
Do you readily become orderless unless you are
strained?
questions from Japanese medical form

If you are given instructions by the doctor, it is imperative
that you carefully follow the directions to the, er, letter.

If you want to do a vowel movement don't stop.
patient instruction sheet, Japan

Unfortunately, this sometimes may seem a bit daunting.

Adults: 1 tablet 3 times a day until passing away
on French prescription bottle

In some cases, you'll be able to pick up basic over-the-
counter medications. The brand names may differ from
those in your medicine cabinet at home, but they'll reas-
sure you that you'll be feeling "in the pink" in no time.

Grow Up Ill
children's medicine, China

Jumping Vitamins: You can't keep them down!
slogan, Indian medication

If you find yourself getting confused by the various brand names, just read the labels for help. They'll tell you everything you need to know.

Known to cure itching, colds, stomachs, brains, and other diseases.
claim on Chinese medicine label

8ml Ear Drops
For the treatment of Ear Affection
Indonesian eardrops

Expiration date: 2 years
medication label, China

Should you opt for traditional, more natural treatments as an alternative to "Westernized" medicine, we offer you one word of warning: Often a little research is advisable, as traditional medicinals can have confusing, difficult-to-understand names and uses.

Section 10
Slender Roll of Medicated Paper
It is a form of preparation made by twisting medicated paper into a slender roll or by twisting

paper into a slender toll and then medicating it, so it is called "slender roll of medicated paper."
> *from* Prescriptions of Traditional Chinese Medicine *by the Shanghai College of Traditional Medicine*

You may be sent to a specialist. Be reassured that the quality of care will be high, if sometimes *unorthodox* (or should we say Protestant?).

Teeth extracted by the latest Methodists
> *advertisement for Hong Kong dentist*

Specialist in women and other diseases
> *sign in doctor's office, Rome*

DR. BLOCK OF BARARAIA
Preventing General Revitalization from stress and ageing and Regeneration
> *newspaper ad, Thailand*

PAKORN CLINIC
Plastic Surgery & General Disease
> *sign in Pattaya, Thailand*

Suggestive Advice on male and female problems; Dr. Vasdev Abbott
> *doctor's ad, Bombay*

But you can relax, knowing that you'll be in good hands.

Yelling Dental Clinic
dentist's office, Taipei, Taiwan

Speaking of dentists, just because you're on vacation doesn't mean you should take a vacation from routine tooth care. Yes, we're talking about using that old standby, dental gross.

> Pull another end of gross and put along the ditch gap of bow-finger and turn up to get down along another bow-finger then return to button on the center.
>> *directions for Japanese tooth flosser (grosser), with accompanying motto: "Help you use gross smoothly and clean tooch dirt"*

Just as in the United States, you can often find useful "medical arts" establishments, offering you more than one form of expert specialist care under one roof.

Colonic
and
Dental Clinic
> *sign, Quezon City, Philippines*

Dental Technician & Dealer in Brassware, Handcrafts and Curios
> *sign on store, Kandy, Sri Lanka*

Dental Clinic by Family Planning Association
> *newspaper ad, Sri Lanka*

You may be surprised at how cutting-edge and advanced medical techniques are.

> Two Sri Lankans get back sight from eyes do-
> nated by world's first woman
> > *headline*, Indonesian Observer

Not to mention how groundbreaking medical research is . . .

THE DEAD AND THE SURVIVED

After one year, among the 141 patients studied in the first phase, 37 were dead. The dead and the survived were compared in terms of various aspects of functioning. It was found that, in all five dimensions of functioning, the dead were generally weaker. The dead had poorer self-perceived economic conditions. More of them thought that their economic resources were not adequate for them to make ends meet. They also had poorer self-perceived mental and physical health conditions. More of them reported deterioration in these conditions during the past 12 months.

The dead also demonstrated a higher level of anxiety than the survived as they found life dull and had more worries. More dead patients had been hospitalized and experienced disablement than the survived.

By and large, fewer dead patients had been able to perform activities to maintain an independent household e.g. moving around, preparing meal, doing household work and washing light clothings. Finally, the dead patients had fewer social contacts and more of them were living alone than the survived.

Hong Kong Polytechnic report

Then again, perhaps you shouldn't be surprised, since doctors abroad, just as back home, must deal with unusual emergency cases all the time . . .

Zaini suffered a five-centimeter cut on his right hand and eight centimeter wound on his left neck.

New Straits Times, *Malaysia*

If an ambulance is necessary, you will discover that they are readily available at any hour you can imagine (and even some you can't).

There are ambulances of general medicine which work from 7-22 o'clock and ambulance on the city stadium is opened from 8-23 o'clock.

sign, Split, Croatia

And what if a "new tourist" wants to emerge when you are overseas? Should you find yourself going into labor in another country, again, we suggest a visit to the nearest hospital—where you, the mother, will receive useful and easy-to-follow instructions.

❋ Strain yourself or push at the time of contrac-tion and two hours later a baby will come out.
❋ A swell will be checked if there is, by pushing shin.
❋ If your weight gains rapidly, it is a sign of swell or fatness.
❋ After you vomit, you rinse your mouse and if you can eat, eat.
❋ Brasure can be for maternity one or nursing bra, so that your breast can't be oppressed.
❋ There are many differences of ideas in family but she felt family bondage after delivery as a wife.

> *from pamphlet for expectant mothers, Public Health Center, Joetsu City, Japan*

One final note: Should you want to *avoid* the arrival of said new tourist, you can always visit the local pharmacy for ironclad protection.

Bullet Proof Condoms
> *condom brand, Sierra Leone*

The Business Traveler

Let us now take a minute to explore the specific needs of the business traveler, who may face different situations from those of the tourist.

First of all, you'll probably want a specialized business hotel. These typically come with all the amenities you'll need—some even complimentary fellow citizens, as it were . . .

The business hotel in the Center of Bangkok, near Shopping Center, Business Area, Computer Market and Garment Market

May we remind you that a relaxed business traveler is a *successful* business traveler . . . and suggest a little pleasure before business?

Now let's get to work! Take a look at the various situations that you, the business traveler, may be facing.

SPECIAL SITUATION #1: Addressing a Group of Foreign Clients or Investors
This is one case where good ol' American humor can really break the ice. Rest assured, your audience will truly appreciate your wit.

American businessman is beginning speech with thing called joke. I am not certain why, but all American businessmen believe it necessary to start speech with joke. [Pause] He is telling joke now, but, frankly, you wouldn't understand it, so I won't translate it. He thinks I am telling you the joke now. [Pause] The polite thing to do when he finishes is to laugh. [Pause] He is getting close. [Pause] Now! [Audience laughs and gives speaker standing ovation]

> *translator for top insurance-company executive who was delivering a speech in Japan in the '80s. Note: After giving the speech, the executive went to the translator and thanked him, saying, "You are the first translator who knows how to tell a good joke."*

SPECIAL SITUATION #2: Attending Trade Shows, Exhibitions, Etc.

There are many trade shows and exhibitions for businesspeople. Some are *very* specialized.

Faeces Expo Osaka

> *sign advertising special exhibition of feces in Osaka, Japan. Representative Shinichi Sakimoto commented to the press, "This is a serious education event."*

Others are quite novel.

Ekspo RealEstat
Guaranteed Free Fictitious Developer

> *from Jakarta trade fair*

This is a wonderful opportunity to get a "hands-on" feel for the types of products and services offered by your international hosts. (You may be pleasantly surprised at the range of products and services you'll find!)

Equipment for Orgasms
> *sign in Otis Engineering exhibit, Moscow—*
> *apparently a mistranslation of "completion*
> *equipment"*

Or not so pleasantly surprised . . .

Keep your Anus clean—Taisho Pharmaceutical
Co. has—marketed a cleansing foam agent, "I
like cleanliness." . . . The "I like clenliness"
whose soft foam contains sterilising agent and
shark lever elements, not only sterilises, but . . .
> *new product, written up in Japanese magazine*
> Diamond Industria

Ningle Brand Piss and Shit Assistant Device
> *product from Nanjing, China*

. . . Or fascinated by new business synergies . . .

Mando Machinery Corporation is the undis-
puted leader in Korea automotive pants industry.
> *press release from a South Korean firm*

Or simply baffled.

Our goal is to develop and persue a simple idea: "to
take up spaces unattainable by other materials".
Once more an italian product, "STONIT" is

brought on the market of outstanding esthetics
and advanced technology.
STONIT is, above all, "itself", far from seeking
to imitate conventional stones.
Stone Italiana, first producer has been playing
for many years now in this field the role proper to
all "NUMBER ONE".'

> *press release, Italy*

You may receive correspondence on interesting new business opportunities . . .

Dear Sir: Due to this reason, we would like to re-
quest your good office that you will give me, au-
thorized, about lot to get pench in side in my lot,
if just will you give me, opportunity, to make a
pench. Just around is in the lot of me.

> *business letter received by Hometown*
> *Development, Philippines*

You'll probably be rubbing elbows with executives from
many dynamic corporations . . .

Complacent Industrial Co., Ltd.
> *Taiwan*

Comatos Computers
> *Dhaka, Bangladesh, cybercafé*

. . . hot new companies . . .

Man On Fire Engineering Co.
Chinese fire-safety equipment company

. . . and those in businesses probably unlike yours . . .

Singer Human Trading Company
Malaysia

. . . subsidiaries you may never have heard of . . .

Sony Young Lavoratory, Inc.
c/o Sony Corporation
inquiry card, Japan

. . . as well as those that may conjure up unintended images . . .

Fuk Hing Business Machines Company
Hong Kong

Wah Hing Precious Screws Factory
China

Lovejoy India
Couplings Quality that guarantees efficiency
ad for New Delhi engineers

Hairichest International Transportation
Hong Kong

And those whose ads seem to be in somewhat . . . *dubious* taste:

> I ♥ cum
> *ad by Locum, Swedish company*

And why not tour local plants and factories? You'll find a ready welcome.

> We earnestly hope that you will not enjoy every one moment of your visit in our Marketing Plaza.
> *letter to visitors to Sanyo, the Japanese electronics firm*

SPECIAL SITUATION #3: Setting Up a Local Office

Setting up a local branch office? Doing business abroad is just the same as doing it at home. You'll find office space—and so much more!—available all around town.

> ARE YOU EXPIRING?
> Diamond Plaza had A-Grade office space.
> Serious inquiries welcome.
> *ad,* Viet Nam News

> Brain for Rent
> *sign on building, Hanoi*

You may need to hire local staff. Why not start with the classifieds?

> Temporarily honest worker in Summit Square.
> Tel: 013-331
> > *ad*, The Malay Mail

But you'll probably have to place an ad yourself to get the perfect person for that position. Before you know it, you'll be inundated with hundreds of employee applications boasting of somewhat unique qualifications:

> This has reference to your advertisement calling for a "typist and an accountant—Male or Female" . . . As I am both for the past several years and I can handle both, I am applying for the post.
> > *cover letter, Kerala, India*

Who knows? You may find that special very *small* and eager-to-work applicant.

> I am enclosed herewith . . .
> > *cover letter with résumé, Kerala, India*

Or those apparently not as eager to work . . .

> Dear Sir, Referring to your current existence in the Indonesian capital market, I think your company has some open vacations.
> > *job-application letter received by Jakarta stockbroker*

And if you can't find the right person to hire, there may be other options . . .

> SOLD: Executive member at Mercantile Club with interesting price. If you are interesting, please call Ms. Anna/Christine at 555.2050 during office hours. Don't miss this chance.
>   *ad*, The Jakarta Post

Should you require expert consulting services, there are always local firms available whose very names inspire confidence.

> The Bozo Research Center, Inc.
>   *Yoyogi-Uehara, Japan*

> Ordinary Engineering Consultant Pte Ltd.
>   *Had Yai, Thailand*

And overseas banking service is usually quite friendly.

> Bank of Overseas Chinese
> Speedy, Infallible, Nice and Overhaul!
> The Bank of Overseas Chinese, the bank of touching!
>   *sign, Taiwan*

Looking to put together that perfect presentation (or should we say persantaion)? You'll need expert English-speaking assistance—and nowadays, overseas, that's easy to come by.

> Staff wanted for Korean Association of Profreaders
> *help-wanted ad, Korea*

> Grammatik proofreads your writing for thousands of writing errors. Incorrent Verb Forms. Infintive usage. Improper sentence construction.
> *ad for proofreading software, Hong Kong*

Perhaps the proofreaders studied at one of the top business schools . . .

> Hitotsubashi Seminar—Hitotsubashi has imordved your study since 1959. That is our mission. It goes without saying that Hitotsubashi is the best. We must work hard for fear that you should fail. We are looking forward to meeting you and studying together.
> *sign advertising business school, Japan*

SPECIAL SITUATION #4: Locating Essential Business Supplies

If you find you've run out of your business cards, not to worry! Just go to a professional printing ship, where skilled technicians will meet your high standards.

> Name Carp Printing
> *business-services sign, Guangzhou, China*

Business Crabs Printed While You Wait
flyer, Cairo

You've got your business cards, now get your business files in order—stylishly.

CLEAR FILE
LUCENT.
CLEAR FILE, put light and superb filing aid,
which perfectly matches your life style . . .
Let this subtle and foppish CLEAR FILE assist
you become a filing expert!
CLEAR FILE, an invaluable partner to your
desk work. Keep it on your desk.
Japanese file

Of course, you'll want the best in all business products. Our advice? Shop around.

Purchase your stock of electronic products, parts,
etc. at high price.
ad fax from Mr. Ho Fax, Hong Kong

Don't throw away your junk. Why not rent more?
ad for Thorn EMI electronics, Japan

Take it to take off away from where other majority has stayed long since. Not only abreast it keeps you but also ahead of the cornfield of computing.

ad for laptop computer, Taiwan

If you purchase sophisticated electronic or telecommunications equipment, you'll be pleased that the instructions usually come in English, explaining the sometimes abstruse technical aspects that might escape you.

Plug the phone jack into the wall. If the phone rings, pick it up and greet the person on the other end by saying "Hello!" or another such greeting. Once completing your conversation, hang up the phone.

instructions for Japanese telephone

Lift the handset.
Dial the telephone number.
Speak to the other party.

instructions for Panasonic phone, Japan

You may also learn computing tips you've never tried before.

Hit mouth two times in rapid succession. Move mouth so curser will appear on moniter.

from Japanese software manual

SPECIAL SITUATION #5: Business Meetings

It is inevitable that at some point or another, you will be meeting with colleagues or clients. Just because you're overseas doesn't mean that you're on "*mañana* time." Punctuality counts! Just make sure your meeting isn't postponed or, for that matter . . .

> Our midday appointment has been pre-poned. Can you please do the needful and get your skates on?
>
> *business phone call, New Delhi*

In fact, often you'll receive an advance notice or . . . something . . . concerning your meeting. (Sometimes you'll receive more than one.)

> We wish to give you advance intimation of our meeting.
>
> *fax, New Delhi ministry office*

> We wish to give you a formal intimation to our meeting.
>
> *follow-up fax, New Delhi ministry office*

> Sir, we would like to confirm our intimation to our meeting.
>
> *invitation card following up the faxes, New Delhi ministry office*

Should you wish to reciprocate, there are many locales where you can entertain and more.

> Grill and Roast your clients! Open for lunch, dinner and Sunday Brunch.
>> *slogan, Hibiscus restaurant in Jakarta Hilton International*

SPECIAL SITUATION #6: Business Etiquette

If you want your business to succeed, it is vital to remember that rules of etiquette often differ overseas, so if you haven't had time to "bone up" on what constitutes proper behavior, just pay attention to instructions and signs.

> Please Flash After Use
>> *sign on toilet stalls in office building, Hong Kong*

> Please don't put anything on the doorknob because it may cause the trouble.
> Administration
>> *sign inside office door, Japan*

> Entrance & Exit for Staff and Impersonator
>> *sign on building, Shanghai*

> No Smorking in Building
>> *sign in Japanese building*

Protocol can be tricky. For example, what do you call that CEO or government official? Some helpful suggestions:

> Position on the Secretary
> ... If you are not sure how you should address me then the following would be considered adequate. . . . .
> Boss
> Namba wan
> Tau bada
> Big Man
> Select whichever you feel comfortable with but not my first name.
>> Paul J. Sail
>> Secretrary
>> Department of Agriculture and Livestock
>> Papua New Guinea

SPECIAL SITUATION #7: Finding a Job

If you've traveled abroad seeking that special position in some overseas paradise, you'll be pleased to find jobs that you never imagined back in Peoria—perfect if you're a "people-person":

> Wanted!! Exhibitionist! More happy and fun people! To join our happy and fun team
>> *help-wanted ad*, Straits Times, *Singapore*

Sales Manager, Area Sales Manager
Must go the whole hog-hug to keep things
going
> *help-wanted ad*, Business India

No limit on sex.
> *help-wanted ad*, The Japan Times *(apparently*
> *trying to say that both male and female*
> *applicants were welcome)*

And don't worry if you're not terribly bright . . .

Vacant English Teachers needed
> *ad*, *South Korean newspaper*

Some of the qualifications, however, might be a little stiff . . .

A fashion company in Kin Bay
Asst. Merchandiser
—neither sex.
> *ad*, *Hong Kong*

. . . and somewhat difficult to meet . . .

COMPANY SECRETARY FINANCE
MANAGER
1) Half-grey haired executives.
2) Must be waist-deep in their field of activities.
3) Must be having the know-how and the do-

how of the latest developments in their respective fields.

> *"Appointments Vacant" listing,* Business India

Other times, flexibility reigns.

> Hyundai Interpretation School would like a spoken English instructor as follows:
> ❊ Qualifications:
> B.A. degree or higher
> ❊ Sex: Male or Female (preferred)
> *help-wanted ad,* Korea Times

Traveler's Tip: Seniors, take note! The job market overseas is often great for older applicants.

> ACCOUNTING MANAGER: Female, not more than 35 years old. CPA, with at least 305 years' experience.
> *help-wanted ad,* JobsDB, *Philippine website*

Customs do vary, so it is wise to be sure you *really* want the job you're applying for.

> Failed applicants will not be returned.
> *recruitment ad for Saigon Marriott Hotel, Ho Chi Minh City, Vietnam*

Finally, a quick note on the business press: Your best source for business and financial information and ideas is the local business newspaper or magazine. Crackerjack business journalists can give you that unique insight that makes all the difference . . .

Congrations to the Business Chronicle
  ad, Manila Chronicle

. . . uncover stories you can't find elsewhere . . .

Korea Green Cross Wins Exclusive Rights to Diarrhea
  headline, Korean Economic Weekly

. . . and perhaps point to ultimate truths.

Dollar Falls in NY
God Higher
  headline, Indonesian Times

Government Agencies and Officials

It's always helpful—especially for those traveling on behalf of their business or government—to get to know local and national officials of the host country.

Government officials, of course, are essentially the same the world over.

At least 1,353 people, mostly government officials, their families and prostitutes, fled Tual on Sunday.

newspaper story, The Jakarta Post

Wherever you go, you'll find that government officials all have that familiar deft way with words and analysis.

> The power of the head of state is not unlimited. Why is it said the power of the President is not unlimited? Probably the idea comes from the English translation: "Is not unlimited."
>
> *Kharis Suhud, speaker of Indonesian*
> *Parliament, in 1988 TV interview*

> Average monthly income receivers income and percentage of income receivers by income receivers income and percentage income receivers and sector.
>
> *title of chart sent to USAID by government of*
> *Sri Lanka*

But often you need *details* about the government officials you'll be dealing with. One way, and dare we say the best way, to familiarize yourself with them is to click on the government's official website—written, of course, in English that you can understand. There you'll find useful biographies of all the top politicos, including their résumés, political positions, and educational attainments. Often you'll be surprised at how little you know about the people you'll be meeting.

> Gianfranco Fini. National Secretary of the Forehead of the Youth . . . expert of the Cones.

Rocco Buttiglione: He has studied jurisprudence . . . under the guide of Prof. the Augosto Of the Walnut . . .

Paolo Bonaiuti: Passes to the "Stone Day." Responsible of Image of Italy force, is megaphone of the President.

Lucio Stanca: Been born to Lucera 20 October, 1941. Conjugated and it has two daughters . . . It has covered loads with President of IBM. Member . . . of the University Mouthfulls.

Mirko Termaglia: It is married with mrs. Italy. Elected to the Room.

Gianni Letti: Been born to Avezzano, 15 April 1935. After to have practised for some years in the professon forense, in the legal study of the father, it passed to militant journalism . . . Head of the press . . . of Knights of the Job . . . He has cured and culvert rubriche TV, in particular on Channel 5.

Umberto Bossi. Been born, 1941. Conjugated, 4 sons. In 1979 enters into contact with the world and ne she becomes the flagman . . . Journalist, is founding of various various journalistic heads and average . . . he comes to an agreement himself with the Pole of Freedoms.

from the official website of the Italian government (www.governo.it.)— since removed

The Local Media

Reading local media is a wonderful way to get your finger on the pulse of your host country. So forget your *Newsweek* or *Time* magazine, and pick up the latest issue of what the locals read. You can get the "happening" news—*before* it makes CNN.

> N. Korean Leader Names Ancient Frog "Ancient Frog"
> *headline*, Bangkok Post

You'll read editorials that are hard-hitting . . .

There may occur eventualities.
> *editorial in the* Korea Times *about the dangers South Korea faces from North Korea*

. . . and eye-opening.

How many more gruesome reports of transvestites committed against human beings will emerge from Burma before the world community disengages from it altogether?
> *editorial,* Bangkok Sunday Post

You can get vivid—sometimes too vivid—pictures of what's "moving" in government and industry . . .

MOTION CARRIED AT DIARRHEA MEETING
> *headline,* Vientiane Times, *Laos*

. . . or with the weather . . .

DOWNPOURS BATTER NATION. GUTS HIT SEOUL STREETS.
> *headline,* Korean Herald

In fact, you'll probably find that the weather coverage overseas meets the same high standards we expect at home.

We are unable to announce the weather. We depend on weather reports from the airport, which is closed, due to the weather. Whether we will be able to give you the weather tomorrow will depend on the weather.

    Arab News, *Jidda, Saudi Arabia*

An oppressive heat wave passed over Calcutta yesterday. In the city the temperature rose to the record figure of about 108 degrees. This sudden rise of temperature was responsible for the intolerable heat.

    Malaysian newspaper

Reading the foreign press, you'll gain valuable insights into scientific and sociological research that might not make the papers back in the U.S., U.K., or Australia, for some reason.

Sociologists have concluded private life depends on money . . .

    Pravda, *Russia*

The inquiry shows that there is no sex in prosperous countries. First of all, this applies to Italy and Germany.

    Pravda, *Russia*

You'll be amazed at the international "flavor" even basic news stories can have.

Banana to serve one-year term, sodomy appeal turned down
headline, New Straits Times, *Malaysia*

And the level of journalism is nonpareil—quantum-mechanically speaking . . .

Continued from tomorrow
subheadline on story in The Island, *Sri Lanka*

And nonpareil in general . . .

Woman's body found in graveyard
The Rising Nepal

Bad weather and frog were allegedly the main reasons of the accident.
Business Vietnam

Let's have spontaneous fun—and here's how.
Straits Times, *Singapore*

Never pour tea directly into your eyes.
helpful hints listed in the Bangkok Post

Even the classified ads are engaging.

Information wanted as to the whereabouts of Mrs. J. O. Plonk (Blonk) wife of J. O. Plonk (Clonk).
advertisement, Chinese newspaper

Where, indeed, is Mrs. Plonk (Blonk)?

Often papers will feature serialized stories by top foreign authors—complete with exciting out-of-this world climaxes that make all that reading well worth the effort.

> He smiled and let his gaze fall to hers, so that her cheek began to glow. Ecstatically she waited until his mouth slowly neared her own. She knew only one thing: rdoeniadtrgoveniard-goverdgovnrdgog.
>
> Badische Presse, *Germany*

Yes, sometimes you may find the typographical standards a bit "off"—but read carefully and you'll get clear insights into their "take" on world affairs.

> London, (AP). Misy J orld2 Iceland's Hofi Karlsdhair xiz to Gyekjavpl hn Fripbya wion a smil p mzssaage for Soviet Leader Mikhwil Gorsachee and Ul.S Pgzxident Gonald Reagwn whom she hoces to meets.
>
> "It's a pewceful vhagntrif . . ." she ywid.
>
> Indonesian Times

For the crossword buff, no need to pine for the *Times*. Many papers carry crossword puzzles in English; fewer, however, seem to carry the answers.

CROSSWORD PUZZLER:

Correction: Today we carry the answer for Saturday's Crossword Puzzler. Answer for today's Puzzler was already printed yesterday. Our readers will find the answer of yesterday's Puzzler tomorrow. The editor regrets the error.

The Jakarta Post

Traveler's Tip: Check out the media notes column of the local paper, if possible, to get ideas of upcoming events that most tourists might not ordinarily hear about.

Media Advisory

Attention: Manila Reporters and Photographers

Around 300 families will be demolished tomorrow, July 3, at 8:00 in the morning

Please come for the event.

press release, Manila newspaper

You may also get *enlightening* insights on famous sports stars.

It was always a delight to be in Pali's company. "Life is too short to be grim always," Pali used to say mockingly, but never quite getting the approval of his charming wife who was always worried about her husband's filament.

obituary of cricket star Kripal Singh in India's Sunday Observer

Reading the local stories, you'll also get interesting ideas you may want to take back home with you.

> When I have stress, I stage a mock pro-wrestling bout with my husband. My favorite technique is to kick him in the groin. When I get a good kick in I really feel happy that I am married.
>
> *Japanese wife quoted in* The Japan Times

Or not.

Finally, take a look at how news from back home is covered. We guarantee you'll get a truly unique angle on history and current events.

> "One small step for man, one giant leap for mankind . . ." Powerful first words from Louis Armstrong, U.S. Astronaut and first man on the moon.
>
> Silicon India *magazine*

So You're Planning to Live Overseas

Perhaps you've been relocated overseas. Or have fallen in love with your foreign paradise and have decided to live there permanently. Or you're in the market for a vacation home. Buying a home overseas is much like buying a home back in the States. But, of course, there are differences.

In many places, the housing market can be rather tight.

> FOR RENT: Condom
> Only US $650
>> *ad*, The Jakarta Post

In others, rather . . . *easy.*

> Come on my house
>> *TV ad for house-building company, Japan*

In addition, you might find that real estate agents don't necessarily do business the way they do at home.

> Live in the most private part of Jakarta in a spacious, luxury apartment set in 5 hectares of secluded gardens. Inspect our private parts today!
>> *ad for apartments, Jakarta*

> This Property is Not for Sale
> For Inquiries call
> E.G. Aguirre
> Tel. 555-2371
> Fax No. 555-2384
>> *sign, Manila*

You can find apartment complexes catering to *every* type of would-be renter.

> Hua Xiang Apartment Villas and Office Complex warmly welcomes the presence of extinguished guests from abroad.
>> *advertisement, China*

> Luminous Nose
>> *apartment building, Japan*

But rules for apartment living might be a little more strin-
gent than what you're used to.

> Please hold a dog in your arms while walking in
> the lobby
>> *sign in Tokyo apartment-building lobby*

Just like in the U.S., it's not always easy to find friendly,
helpful, professional movers.

> Fuk Yu
>> *moving company, Hong Kong*

And finding the *right* people to help you maintain your
home once you've moved in can be difficult. Their standards may be a bit . . . different . . . from yours.

> House keeping:
> Cleaning, defecating, sterilizing for new resi-
>   dence
> Floor maintaining face-lifting polishing to
>   kitchen and toilet
> Carpet cleaning:
> Clean, defecate, maintain all kinds of carpet
>> *ad for Mei Ao Labour cleaning service in*
>> Beijing Today

> Ah Lai personality doing all plumbing job. Cost
> low so price low. if U need any problems call me.
>> *classified ad*, Straits Times, *Singapore*

But maybe, especially for renters, this won't be a problem.

> Deposit: The owner asks for a deposit of 25.000
> ptas as a guarantee for the flat. This amount will
> be returned at the end of your stay if any damage
> has been done.
>
> *sign in Spanish building*

Shopping for Essentials

The long-term visitor will also need to shop for groceries, detergents, soaps, tissues, and the like. Travelers, rest assured you'll find these everyday items at fine everyday stores, like these supermarkets:

Membrane Supermarket
   China

Super Super Super
   Japan

Just make sure you enter through the right door!

Door No. 1: "Entrance"
Door No. 2: "Exitrance"
supermarket, Azabu, Japan

A stroll down the supermarket aisles will be a fun adventure of sorts.

Aisle A: Caned Fruit
Aisle B: Caned Vegetarian
        Caned Fish Meat
        Dried Meat Floss
Chinese supermarket sign

What enticing product come-ons!

Tahitian Noni: Everyone, Everywhore
slogan for Japanese soft drink

A lovely paper for your toilet life
on toilet-paper wrapping, Japan

Be half as fresh as the day is long
slogan on tampons, Japan

Ghana, is, as you perhaps in Korea, and is regarded as the high-qualified Ghana our marvelous, smooth and mild whole already know, enjoying high reputation selling chocolates masterpieces of all milk chocolate.
slogan on Ghana-brand chocolate bar, Korea

Good morning, dear lemons. How juicy you look today.

label on lemon soft drink, Japan

Rechee Milk Flavor Chips. Use for snack, fun, panties.

Chinese snack-food pack

CIGAR FARM MILK PIE
Ten yards away, a
dandruff of snow sp
rinkling onto their u-
ncovered heads, a d-
ozen or more football
players clasp hands
and kneel in prayee
r not for themselv
es, but for the safety
of brother and siste
rs overseas who have

on Japanese candy-bar wrapper

Present for you delicious taste! Enjoy your happy times with this donut!

on donut package, Japan

Clean dirty ice cream on a wafer-based cone

ad for Clean ice cream, Philippines

This crud is from the finest milk soley from the cow's of the Brie region.
label on French cheese

Too fast to live, too young to happy.
slogan for cream soda, Japan

We doubt you could have put it any better.

Of course, the ads will try the old "hard sell" (or is semi-soft more appropriate?):

Once You Taste It You Will Find It Irresistible For a Second
ad for Sekchimei candy, Macao

One plus: Often, while the brand names are unfamiliar, they're descriptive enough to let you know just what's in that package.

My Fanny
Japanese toilet paper

Other times, however, you might be a little . . . stumped . . .

Telephone
Malaysian agar powder

Battleship
Malaysian canned squid

Quickle
> *Japanese toilet paper*

Foco Pennywort
> *Malaysian soda*

Kabitori Haiter Spray
> *Japanese hair spray*

Angst
> *Vietnamese chicken pâté*

Ban Cock
> *Indian cockroach repellent*

Creap creamy powder
> *Japanese coffee creamer*

Luxury
> *Malaysian crackers*

Snacks Pickle Ex
> *Japanese bourbon-flavored chocolates*

Papal Soap
> *Japanese soap*

Crunky
> *Japanese chocolate bar*

Crundy
Japanese gourmet chocolates

Parrot Toilet
Thai soap

Clean Finger Nail
Chinese tissues

Other times, the product names might conjure up images that we'd rather not . . . er, have conjured up . . .

Last Climax
Japanese tissues

Cat Wetty
Japanese moistened hand towels

Ass Glue
Chinese glue

Blue Peter
Norwegian canned fish

Suck All—Yone's Need Almighty Sucker
Thai "bathroom pads"

My Pee
Japanese napkins

Donkee Basterd Suker
sugar sold in Amsterdam

Along these lines, many laundry detergents seem some-what *unfortunately* named.

Barf
Uzbekistan's top-selling laundry detergent

Polio
Czech Republic laundry detergent

Colon Plus
Spanish detergent

Purge
Indian detergent

Not to mention fertilizers . . .

Green Piles
Japanese lawn fertilizer

As always, you'll find items conveniently displayed, often with helpful product claims in English.

Trade Mark K—Showvels Scoops and Spades which are exhibited of the above trade mark is very cheap in the pice and it is bonvenient bor

Use. There is neceity exclain ally aeknorulebqe
by thebll customers.

sign on display in Japanese housewares store

This floodlight is capable of illuminating large
areas, even in the dark

Komatsu floodlight label, Japan

The cooks among you will, of course, want to check out
kitchenware departments. You'll find unique cooking
equipment with even more unique instructions!

Some times screaming from the inside of the
safety valve, etc., could be, but this does not
mean being out of order at all.

from user's guide, Combi pressure cooker,
Korea

ice of shape Half-circled and flat so that ice
dropout from ice-maker directly that while ice-
making and taking out ice without applying
hands to touch ice. Healthy First!

instructions for Chinese plastic ice-cube tray

Multicooker
Suitable for friend food and deep friend food

ad for kitchen appliance, Jakarta

Plain Mind Coffee Pot It's a nice thing to spend
everyday with one's identity. To hold the iden-

tity, to have one's assertion. Please find yourself
for each nice day.

product label, Japan

With Fresh Vegetables dayly . . . Just a little bit,
    different Tastes of a regular cook.
Helps you in cooking fast, joyful beautiful sharp
    edged!
Made of Safety Type, Hi-Quality Nylon Brin-
    forced Glass
Helps your cooking fast, joyfully with wonder-
    fully edged strings!
Slices, Tine cuts, Strips, etc., made speedily and
    with no wastes.

*instructions on kitchen aid that makes potato
curls, Japan*

Granted, sometimes the instructions may be a bit enigmatic.

Not to be used for the other use

*from Japanese food-processor instruction
manual*

And recipes included with some of these appliances may
be a bit . . . off-putting.

Cooking method: 1) Wash and rape the sweet potato.

>   *from* Qingdao Fisherman Feast of China *by*
>   *Gao Bingyi, described as a "famous special*
>   *cooker"*

Other products offer special dispensations.

The World Highest Quality titanium Alloy Blade
The knife assures special resistance to attrition and permanent freedom from lusting

>   *ad in* Japan Economic Review

Speaking of cooking, home chefs will be surprised at some of the unexpected ingredients found in familiar prepared foods. Truly, shopping (and eating!) abroad is an adventure.

Lard, onion and species

>   *ingredients, Vietnamese specialty pastry*
>   *"mooncakes," as listed by the Vietnam*
>   *National Administration of Tourism*

Orange Drink
made of pure, fresh cow's milk

>   *ad, Malaysia*

Garlic Paste
Ingredients: Fresh Ginger, salt, vinegar

>   *product label, Hong Kong*

Ingredients:
Wheat
Made from Recycled Cardboard
>   *printed on cereal box, Malaysia*

Even the chewing gum has more . . . flair, shall we say?

Shocking gum
Relax gum
Panic gum
Etiquette gum
Gum gum
Booing Blue Cola—super brain panic gum
No Time gum
>   *Japanese gum brands*

You'll also run across some new foods . . .

Four legged Chicken 29.90 Each
>   *Hong Kong supermarket ad*

Even the bottled water is a little different—in terms of
both names *and* claims!

Tepelene Mineral Water
Analyzed for all parameters
suffled how it gush from the source of the woods
of Tepelena
>   *Albanian bottled water*

Kolic
> *Japanese mineral water*

Aqua Mineral—Improved!—Arsenic free
> *label on Bangladeshi bottled water*

Free Bacteria
> *printed on bottles of Vietnamese mineral water*

Caution: This commodity is restricted to drinking purposes only
Aqua-Tek Pure Distilled Water
> *Hong Kong water*

If all of your shopping is getting you tired, why not have a "nosh" to boost your energy level? Pick up a sweet treat for a quick sugar rush—but be careful not to "pig out"!

Swine
> *Chinese chocolate*

Asse chocolate
> *Japanese candy*

There's such a wide range of tasty sweets that sound oh so tempting!

Chocolate Colon
Snot Cookies
> *Japanese cookies*

Plopp
> *Malaysian candy bar*

Used Apple Juice from Aomori
> *on cookie box, Aomori, Japan*

Very Strange Crisp
> *Chinese lollipop*

Natural Come Peanut Milk Candy
> *Shenzen Natural Come Food candy, China*

Non-sugar-eaters need not despair; you can chomp on *these* delectable goodies:

Homo sausage
> *East Asian fish sausage*

Julie's Kaka Crackers
> *Malaysia*

Thailand Peanus
> *Chinese peanuts*

Freeze Dried Gruel
> *food product available in Hong Kong*

Shitto
> *pepper sauce, Ghana*

And wash it all down with a swig of refreshing

Pipi
: *Yugoslavian orangeade*

Zit
: *Greek soft drink*

Gag
: *French soft drink*

If you need a real lift, may we suggest grabbing a six-pack of:

Libido
: *Chinese soda*

And don't worry about the quality. You'll find that food packagers overseas are just as concerned as those back home about health and safety issues—if not more so . . .

> We are specializing in making dried-pork and pork-sliced. . . . The staff is under expert supervision and hygienically packed.
> *Hong Kong label*

Latte lovers, take note: An overseas trip can be a wonderful time to stock up on exciting new coffee brands.

Old Beans
: *Japanese coffee*

Ucc
Japanese coffee

I'm Dripper
Japanese instant coffee

Ease Your Bosoms
*Japanese coffee—intended to be a stress
reducer*

Black coffee has great features which other cof-
fees have never had: Non-sugar.
on Japanese coffee label

Key Coffee: Just add milk to enjoy the genuine
tea taste!
Japanese coffee

Suzuki coffee: Your Last Impression
Japanese coffee

Traveling with Children

Traveling with children can be a challenge, but it can also be a delight. Our advice? Keep the tykes busy while on the road, or in the hotel room, or while sightseeing.

Some tried-and-true "kiddie tips":

Tip #1: Encourage your little ones to write letters to their friends at home. Pick up some cute stationery at that charming local store to get them going.

Little Hussy
Japanese writing tablet for little girls

Young Snot
on cover of Japanese writing pad

Tip #2: If you're going to be overseas for a while, don't neglect their education. You'll find many helpful books, and even teachers.

A,C,B
alphabet book, Japan

PETTY RABBIT by Bettyix Botter
on Chinese thermos

Preparation of Maths and English for Failure in X and XII
advertisement for exam prep school, Indian Express

Gifted children can benefit from a vacation spot fully equipped to keep those junior Einsteins occupied.

To the children is reserved a green play-back and are proposed particular stays with animation and naturalistic didactic-laboratories.
website advertising villa for rent in Trivigno, Italy

Tip #3: Be aware *beforehand* of those special rules regarding children. Does Baby Johnny want to send a letter? Maybe Mommy had better take care of it instead.

Babies Are Not Served
> *sign in Hong Kong post offices*

Children Must Enter with Parrots Only.
> *sign at museum entrance, Madrid*

Children must be accompanied by part of an adult.
> *sign on hotel pool, Bangkok*

Tip #4: If traveling with an infant, don't be concerned if you run out of Gerber or Beech-Nut. There are babies overseas, of course, and they have to eat too!

Ugly Baby
> *Chinese baby food*

Felony
> *Indonesian baby food*

The same applies to baby toiletries.

Mypee
> *Japanese baby shampoo*

Skinababe
> *Japanese baby cleanser*

Not to mention clothing.

Lusty Baby
  Japanese children's clothing line

Tip #5: Of course, there's always time for some play. So pick up a special foreign toy for the kids. What fun they'll have . . . after you've assembled it.

DRAGONBALL Z TOY ASSEMBLY
Setting Pre Ceiling Way and Means:

(1) with appertain rotor of screw setting pre ceiling on the under standing that serew no wield. May wield two-faced, pressboard securing. wied pre to begin with wiping ceiling of bilge dasto.

(2) Thread of length need half as many again as tad.

(3) Open toy of batteries shuck. Verification batteries,+,− whereafter stow down.to a certainty need locknat lest take place accident.

(4) Hook through toys apside of hole.

(5) Needs swithes shoving NO.for pre arrows specifying of orention shoving. Pack it up time, withbold toy pate,need switches shoving OFF.

✻ Prythee no sport with stingy or play asperity game. Winding finger have got bloodstream not wallk. Throagh of peril.

✻ Tad disport of time grown man tatelage.

✻ Till the cowcomes home.Wield toys damage, burn-in prythee wind to a close wield.

✻ Give attention to open/close toys,therefore

take place peril.for instance slipup batteries wield result in the emission of heat rupture liquid.vent itself prythee pay attention.

❋ Play at sith to a certainty bolt up power supply fetch out batteries.

❋ Batteries no electification dissolution,plunge ioto aquaor fire.

❋ Not trust for tad batteries lest in advertent eat off. In the event of accident without loss of time plythee pillroller tuke order with.

May pre house the seamy side volitation!!!

> *instructions and warnings on Dragonball Z*
> *toy, Japan*

"Qimiao" top is an intellectual toy made auording to physical fundamentals, it has simple stmcture, advanced technological procese, delicate model and various ways to play. It inspires children's thacghts and touches off the latent energy of scientific knowledge. Deep individually the friends welcome.

MANIPULATION INSTNUTIONS:
To start with the rack: Make the rack tallywith the wheel, Then pull it out with ease, make the top rotate at a high speed.
To start with the thread: wind the thread around the axis, hold the outside circle of the top with left hand, peass thelong end of the thread with

the left palm, draw out the short amd of the thread with force, make the top rotate at the high speed.

A life seems to bave been poured into the rotafing toy as soom as it gets started. LED will rmit light and form a colorful circle, NO inatter where it is or what angle it is at, the toy may always stand wpright, lay down, It is veny enyoyable, Many diggicult and exciting plays can be xomplets during the process.

instructions on top made in China

Can't invert with laugh.
The laugh begin. you are youthful.
Automatize.
As poke as shaky as shaky as laugh.
During the use, open the lid of top and take two cells (No. 5) in the box. If you want stop laugh or don't use for a long time, you must take out the cells (this seller have no cells)

printed on box of Vietnamese top that giggles
and laughs

Be sure the toys you buy are safe and age-appropriate.

DANGER!
A dangerous toy. This toy is being made for the extreme priority the good looks. The little part which suffocates when the sharp part which gets hurt is swallowed is contained generously. Only

the person who can take responsibility by itself is
to play.

> *warning label, Japanese toy*

Tip #6: If, for some reason, that toy never gets assembled,
pick up fun souvenir clothing at a children's boutique.

> Junior Poisoning
> > *children's clothing shop, Tokyo*

The clothing often comes complete with cute slogans in
real English!

> We are all prostitutes to please you.
> > *on children's T-shirt, Tokyo*

> NOBODY KNOWS WHERE IT IS
> THAT'S A DARK AND LONELY PLACE
> > *on pair of little girl's panties decorated with a*
> > *cute panda bear, birds, and flowers, Japan*

Tip #7: When all else fails and Mom and Dad really need
to get some time alone, why not call your local

> BABY SHITTER—I take care of your children.
> Please call up me.
> > *sign in Tokyo*

Travel Etiquette

A few quick words about etiquette abroad. Remember, when you're overseas, you are an ambassador of your home country. So please keep a check on your spitting and vomiting!

> Please Do Not Spit Too Long. Thank you.
> *sign, Malaysia*

> It (vomit) causes inconvenience when you are passing by and walking down the street.
> *reason given by officials in Philippine city who*
> *passed an ordinance against public vomiting,*
> *as printed in the* Philippine Daily Inquirer

Do not spit here and there.
>   *sign, Calcutta*

Not to mention other bodily issuances.

Commit no urinating and shitting at random.
>   *warning notice, Shenzhen Municipal City,*
>   *China*

Or almost everything else.

Don't squat when waiting for a bus or a person.
Don't spit in public. Don't point at people with
your fingers. Don't make noise. Don't laugh
loudly. Don't yell or call to people from a dis-
tance. Don't pick your teeth, pick your nose,
blow your nose, pick at your ears, rub your eyes,
or rub dirt off your skin. Don't scratch, take off
your shoes, burp, stretch or hum.
>   *government-issued list of traveler's tips, China*

In other words . . .

Commit No Nuisance.
>   *sign, Calcutta*

Of course, you're in a foreign country, so sometimes the
rules may seem a little . . . opaque.

Please take off your shoes and keep them in this chapel before they are invisible.

> *sign in wat, Bangkok*

Please do not be a dog.

> *sign on grass in Paris park*

No Paraphernalia

> *sign next to group of benches in Happy Valley, Hong Kong*

Remember, what "they" say overseas might not be what *you* think they're saying . . .

. . . when they said, "Your sister is very ugly and very stupid," what they meant was "Sir, I am afraid your sister is fairly attractive and ravishing." Korean words meaning "nice looking" are also synonymous with "ugly" and so is the word "smart" standing in for "stupid."

> *Kim Young Wha, patriotic Korean lecturer who objected to a visiting teacher's remarking that the teacher's students had told him his sister was ugly and stupid*

About the Authors

KATHRYN PETRAS and ROSS PETRAS are siblings and the authors of the national bestselling "Stupidest" series as well as other humor books. Their titles include *Unusually Stupid Americans, The 776 Stupidest Things Ever Said, Stupid Sex,* and *Very Bad Poetry.* Their work has received the attention of such diverse personalities as David Brinkley and Howard Stern and publications including *The New York Times, Playboy, The Wall Street Journal, The Washington Post,* and the London *Times,* and has been featured on numerous television networks, including ABC, CBS, NBC, and CNN. They are also the creators of the number one bestselling *365 Stupidest Things Ever Said Page-A-Day Calendar* (now in its eleventh year).